# ANCIENT EGYPT

## THE LAND AND ITS LEGACY

T.G.H. JAMES

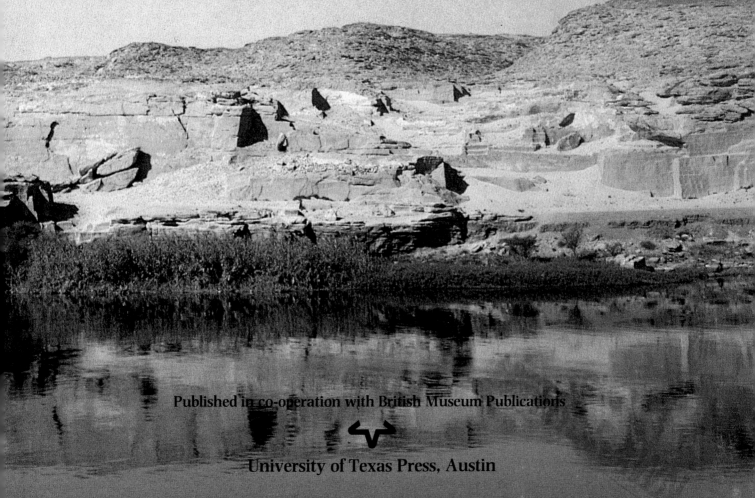

Published in co-operation with British Museum Publications

University of Texas Press, Austin

International Standard Book Number:
0-292-72062-9 (cloth)
0-292-70426-7 (paperback)
Library of Congress Catalog Card Number 87-51646
Copyright © 1988 T.G.H. James

First University of Texas Press Paperback Printing, 1990

Requests for permission to reproduce material
from this work should be sent to Permissions,
University of Texas Press, Box 7819, Austin,
Texas 78713-7819

Designed by Roger Davies
Phototypeset in Monotype Photina Series 747
by Southern Positives and Negatives (SPAN),
Lingfield, Surrey
and printed and bound in Italy

**Half-title page** Osiris with the features of
Hatshepsut. One of a number of representations
of the queen from her temple at Deir el-Bahri,
now in the Metropolitan Museum of Art, New
York.

**Title page** The west bank of the Nile at Gebel es-
Silsila; some of the smaller sandstone quarries
can be seen lying behind the line of entrances to
the shrines.

**This page** The fortified heights of Qasr Ibrim; a
view taken before the filling of Lake Nasser.

# CONTENTS

# CHRONOLOGICAL TABLE
## *(with selected monarchs)*

The system of dating used in this volume follows that adopted in J. Baines and J. Málek, *Atlas of Ancient Egypt*.

**Early Dynastic Period**
(DYNASTIES I–II)
*First Dynasty*
*Second Dynasty*
c. 2920–2649 BC

**Old Kingdom**
(DYNASTIES III–VIII)
*Third Dynasty*
c. 2649–2575 BC
Djoser
c. 2630–2611 BC
*Fourth Dynasty*
c. 2575–2465 BC
Snofru
c. 2575–2551 BC
Cheops (Khufu)
c. 2551–2528 BC
Mycerinus (Menkaure)
c. 2490–2472 BC
Shepseskaf
c. 2472–2467 BC
*Fifth Dynasty*
c. 2465–2323 BC
Sahure
c. 2458–2446 BC
Neferirkare
c. 2446–2426 BC
Djedkare Isesi
c. 2388–2356 BC
Unas
c. 2356–2323 BC
*Sixth Dynasty*
c. 2323–2150 BC
Meryre Pepi I
c. 2289–2255 BC
Neferkare Pepi II
c. 2246–2152 BC
*Seventh Dynasty*
*Eighth Dynasty*
c. 2150–2134 BC

**First Intermediate Period**
(DYNASTIES IX–X)
*Ninth Dynasty*
*Tenth Dynasty*
c. 2134–2040 BC
Kings named Akhtoy (Khety), Merikare

**Middle Kingdom**
(DYNASTIES XI–XII)
*Eleventh Dynasty*
c. 2134–1991 BC
*Wahankh Inyotef II*
c. 2118–2069 BC
Nebhepetre Mentuhotpe II
c. 2061–2010 BC
*Twelfth Dynasty*
c. 1991–1783 BC
Sehetepibre Ammenemes I
c. 1991–1962 BC
Kheperkare Sesostris I
c. 1971–1926 BC
Nubkaure Ammenemes II
c. 1929–1892 BC
Khakheperre Sesostris II
c. 1897–1878 BC
Khakaure Sesostris III
c. 1878–1841 BC
Nymare Ammenemes III
c. 1844–1797 BC

**Second Intermediate Period**
(DYNASTIES XIII–XVII)
*Thirteenth Dynasty*
c. 1783–1633 BC
Sekhemre Sewadjtowy Sobkhotpe III
c. 1744–1741 BC
Khasekhemre Neferhotep I
c. 1741–1730 BC
*Fourteenth Dynasty*
c. 1786–1603 BC
*Fifteenth Dynasty*
(Hyksos)
c. 1674–1550 BC
*Sixteenth Dynasty*
c. 1684–1550 BC
*Seventeenth Dynasty*
c. 1640–1550 BC
Nubkheperre Inyotef VI
c. 1640–1635 BC
Sobkemsaf I
c. 1642–1626 BC

**New Kingdom**
(DYNASTIES XVIII–XX)
*Eighteenth Dynasty*
c. 1550–1307 BC
Nebpehtyre Amosis I
c. 1550–1525 BC
Djeserkare Amenophis I
c. 1525–1504 BC
Akheperkare Tuthmosis I
c. 1504–1492 BC
Akheperenre Tuthmosis II
c. 1492–1479 BC

Makare Hatshepsut
c. 1473–1458 BC
Menkheperre Tuthmosis III
c. 1479–1425 BC
Akheprure Amenophis II
c. 1427–1401 BC
Menkheprure Tuthmosis IV
c. 1401–1391 BC
Nebmare Amenophis III
c. 1391–1353 BC
Neferkheprure Amenophis IV (Akhenaten)
c. 1353–1335 BC
Ankhkheprure Smenkhkare
c. 1335–1333 BC
Nebkheprure Tutankhamun
c. 1333–1323 BC
Kheperkheprure Ay
c. 1323–1319 BC
Djeserkheprure Horemheb
c. 1319–1307 BC
*Nineteenth Dynasty*
c. 1307–1196 BC
Menpehtyre Ramesses I
c. 1307–1306 BC
Menmare Sethos I
c. 1306–1290 BC
Usermare Ramesses II
c. 1290–1224 BC
Baenre Merenptah
c. 1224–1214 BC
Userkheprure Sethos II
c. 1214–1204 BC
*Twentieth Dynasty*
c. 1196–1070 BC
Usermare-Meryamun Ramesses III
c. 1194–1163 BC
Hiqmare Ramesses IV
c. 1163–1156 BC
Nebmare Ramesses VI
c. 1151–1143 BC

**Late Dynastic Period**
(DYNASTIES XXI–XXX)
*Twenty-first Dynasty*
c. 1070–945 BC
*Twenty-second Dynasty*
c. 945–712 BC
Hedjkheperre Sheshonq I
c. 945–924 BC
Osorkon I
c. 924–909 BC
Usermare Osorkon II
c. 883–855 BC
Pimay
c. 783–773 BC

*Twenty-third Dynasty*
c. 828–712 BC
*Twenty-fourth Dynasty*
c. 724–712 BC
*Twenty-fifth Dynasty*
c. 750–657 BC
Piankhi (Piye)
c. 750–712 BC
Neferkare Shabaka
c. 712–698 BC
Khunefertemre Taharqa
c. 690–664 BC
*Twenty-sixth Dynasty*
c. 664–525 BC
Wahibre Psammetichus I
c. 664–610 BC
Wehemibre Necho II
c. 610–595 BC
Neferibre Psammetichus II
c. 595–589 BC
Haibre Wahibre (Apries)
c. 589–570 BC
Khnemibre Amosis II (Amasis)
c. 570–526 BC
*Twenty-seventh Dynasty*
c. 525–404 BC
*Twenty-eighth Dynasty*
c. 404–399 BC
*Twenty-ninth Dynasty*
c. 399–380 BC
*Thirtieth Dynasty*
c. 380–343 BC
Kheperkare Nectanebo I
c. 380–362 BC
Snedjemibre Nectanebo II
c. 360–343 BC

**Macedonian Kings**
c. 332–305 BC
Alexander the Great
c. 332–323 BC
Philip Arrhidaeus
c. 323–317 BC

**Ptolemaic Kings**
c. 305–30 BC
Ptolemy I Soter I
c. 305–282 BC
Ptolemy V Epiphanes
c. 205–180 BC
Ptolemy VIII Euergetes II
c. 170–116 BC
Cleopatra VII Philopator
c. 51–30 BC

*(Opposite)* Sunrise at Giza.

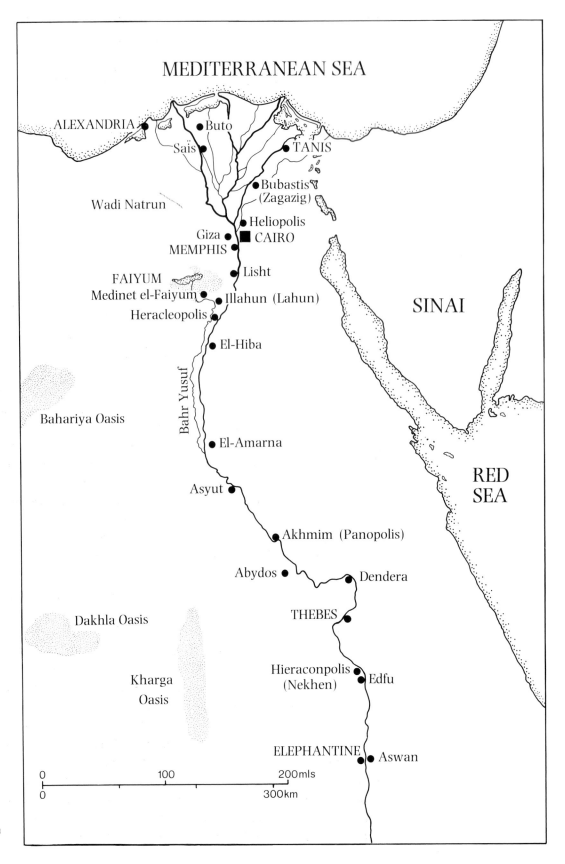

MEDITERRANEAN SEA

ALEXANDRIA

Buto

Sais

TANIS

Bubastis
(Zagazig)

Wadi Natrun

Heliopolis

Giza

CAIRO

MEMPHIS

Lisht

FAIYUM

Medinet el-Faiyum

Illahun (Lahun)

Heracleopolis

El-Hiba

SINAI

Bahr Yusuf

Bahariya Oasis

El-Amarna

Asyut

RED
SEA

Akhmim (Panopolis)

Abydos

Dendera

Dakhla Oasis

THEBES

Kharga

Oasis

Hieraconpolis
(Nekhen)

Edfu

ELEPHANTINE

Aswan

0            100         200mls
0                    300km

Egypt from the Mediterranean
Sea to the First Cataract.

# The Unknown Land

## THE DELTA

MOST PEOPLE who visit Egypt these days arrive by air in Cairo, whether they come on business or as tourists. Egypt seems to begin at Cairo, and the natural direction to turn is southwards – up the Nile by boat or train, or even again by air, to Luxor and to Aswan and to points between. The visitor by air is aware of crossing a coast after the flight over the Mediterranean. Usually the aeroplane flies over desert until the massive spread of Cairo appears; sometimes it passes over green cultivation, marked by numerous small towns and villages, but without other remarkable features apart from the glittering lines of river-branch or canal. Anticipation of arrival, and the possible view of the pyramids as the plane circles round Cairo, concentrate attention on what is to come and not on what may be glimpsed from twenty thousand feet through haze and fleeting cloud.

And yet, north of Cairo lies the greater part of inhabited Egypt, the fan-shaped Delta, an inverted triangle of dense farmland, an area which is neglected today by tourist and even archaeologist (with a few notable exceptions). Because it is a land of waterways it has always been difficult of access. Roads until recently were undeveloped and seemed mostly to go in directions other than those required by the adventurous traveller. To go from east to west in the northern Delta remains an adventure, involving many irksome detours and much back-tracking.

In ancient times the solution to travel in the Delta lay in the branches of the Nile which served as obvious and convenient highways, just as the mainstream of the river provided the best means of communication between the ancient metropolis of Memphis, just south of the Delta's apex, and Elephantine, at the southernmost boundary of Egypt. It was along the same waterways that visitors to Egypt in modern times passed through the Delta to Cairo before the coming of the aeroplane and the cutting of the Suez Canal. Alexandria was the point of arrival, and in those days of leisurely travel it was a place in which to pause for a few days before undertaking the sail by felucca or dahabiya (houseboat) to Cairo and Shepheard's Hotel.

In almost every respect the nineteenth-century traveller to Egypt was at an advantage compared with today's two-week visitor. It would, however, be disingenuous to pretend that the early Victorian sailing up to Cairo along canals and the Rosetta branch of the Nile would have seen much of antiquity or felt the need to stop to wander about the ruined mounds of unnamed but romantic cities. Nevertheless, the early visitors, in the years subsequent to the opening of Egypt to Europeans after the disastrous Napoleonic expedition of 1798–1801, had a more general curiosity about the whole of Egypt, and usually the time to spend in quartering the Delta as well as ranging the Nile Valley to the south of Cairo. In this respect it is curious to note that Baedeker's first Egyptian guide book, published in 1878, dealt only with the Delta, Sinai and Cairo with its environs. The rest of the Nile Valley would follow only in 1892. A recently published guide, which reflects in its treatment of sites the priorities of the modern visitor, devotes fewer than 20 pages to the Delta out of 246 for the whole country.

It is not surprising that early visitors approached Egypt and its monuments with almost as much apprehension as curiosity. Here was a true *terra incognita*, known, if at all, only from the writings of classical authors, of Herodotus, of Plutarch, of Diodorus Siculus and, geographically, of Strabo in particular. The few Egyptian antiquities which had reached Europe in modern times, putting on one side the obelisks and other pieces of monumental sculpture brought to Rome during the Empire but still visible in the city, were almost without exception very much of the 'curiosity' category – mummies and small inexplicable figures of daemons in bronze and faience, regularly called 'idols' by early collectors and antiquaries. There was an almost complete lack of understanding. It now seems perverse to judge things Egyptian by classical standards, but the tendency to do so still persists to some extent. The discreet voyeur in the Egyptian gallery of any large museum will not uncommonly observe a few visitors, unsure of their reactions, standing sideways to a monument, aping what they think to be the Egyptian way of showing the moving figure.

The approach to Egypt, then, was by sea to Alexandria, and much time might be spent in the Delta. So it was certainly for the nineteenth-century Egyptologist, and even for many less dedicated visitors who might be passing several months in Egypt during the winter. Throughout the flat landscape of Lower Egypt, the distant skyline might be interrupted by the extensive mounds which marked the sites of ancient cities. In antiquity the Delta was a land of twenty nomes or provinces, and the nome capitals were religious centres as well as the seats of political power and of provincial bureaucracy. Although some of these cities were of great antiquity – the fame of Buto, for example,

1 A Delta landscape.

2 The theatre at Kom el-Dik in Alexandria.

dates back to before the unification of Upper and Lower Egypt – many were of relatively recent importance. During the later dynasties of the Pharaonic Period, small principalities throughout the Delta achieved prominence and their cities entered into a period of growth and prosperity which continued throughout the last millennium BC and extended into the early centuries AD. A few of these cities remained important inhabited sites through late antiquity, the arrival of Islam in the seventh century AD and the redevelopment of Egypt from the time of Muhammad Ali in the early nineteenth century.

Delta towns like Damanhur, Sa el-Hagar (Saïs) and Benha have histories of occupation which go back for thousands of years. Such places are scarcely available for extensive and systematic archaeological investigation. Other ancient cities like Buto and San el-Hagar (Tanis) were abandoned in late antiquity and have survived only as desolate, if huge, mounds of crumbled mud-brick buildings. Here were the happy hunting grounds of traveller, archaeologist and antiquities dealer, and many sites, undisturbed for 1,500 years or more, were raked over and despoiled of visible antiquities. Almost all the great mounds were also greatly diminished, in some cases with formidable completeness, by local farmers who used the crumbled, mature brickwork as fertiliser on their fields. This last disastrous process, which has certainly not been confined to the Delta, has destroyed a major part of the evidence for ancient Egypt's domestic history. But in the Delta the loss is particularly sad, for it has occurred almost unnoticed and therefore wholly unchecked.

For reasons of accessibility, some of the earliest monuments to leave Egypt came from the Delta, some even from activities which might be described as archaeological. Two large basalt slabs inscribed on both sides for King Psammetichus I of the Twenty-sixth Dynasty (664–610 BC) and for King Nectanebo I of the Thirtieth Dynasty (380–362 BC), are said to have been found in Alexandria. They are called 'inter-columnar', because such slabs were used to fill spaces between columns in temples; they may, however, have

3

3 Inter-columnar slab from a temple in the Delta. King Psammetichus I makes offerings to underworld deities.

4 The Attarine Mosque in Alexandria. The small domed building contained the sarcophagus of King Nectanebo II.

been used to form a low barrier wall. The history of their discovery, although obscure, is curious. Edward Wortley Montagu, a son of the famous Levantine traveller Lady Mary Wortley Montagu, was a man of broad tastes and extravagant, even mad, behaviour. Obliged to leave England for reasons of prudence, he spent some years travelling in Italy, Egypt and the Near East, engaging in both reputable and disreputable activities, the former of which included primitive archaeological researches in the region of Alexandria. His finds were sent back as gifts to his brother-in-law, the third Earl of Bute, who presented the most impressive pieces to George III. Interesting and important though the intercolumnar slabs are to Egyptologists today, and fine though their royal representations of Psammetichus and Nectanebo are, they did not, apparently, greatly please the king, who passed them on, perhaps unseen, to the British Museum which was then but thirteen years old.

Even more curious is the tale surrounding the acquisition of the monumental sarcophagus made of greenish breccia for King Nectanebo II (360–343 BC), the last native ruler of Egypt in antiquity. It also was found in Alexandria, but in very strange circumstances. It had stood for centuries, perhaps since antiquity, in a very public place in the city. Before its removal by the French during the Napoleonic occupation, and subsequently by the British army from the French, it served as a washing basin for the ablutions of worshippers in the Attarine Mosque, and earlier for a similar purpose in a church dedicated to St Athanasius on the same spot. By tradition possibly, but certainly

4

by misidentification, the sarcophagus was ascribed to Alexander the Great and it was under this title that it was included among the collection of antiquities put together by the French scholars who had come to Egypt with Napoleon to set up an institute and to study the country. Here was a real prize to extract from Napoleon's agents and even if it did weigh nearly seven old-fashioned tons, and did measure over ten feet in length, over five feet in width and nearly four feet in height, it was certainly worth taking back to England. In his charming but inconsistent guide to Alexandria, E.M. Forster debits the removal of the great coffin from the mosque – a singular act of impiety – to the British, not the French; but the official French report on the scientific results of the great expedition states quite clearly that 'this fine monument was on board to be transported to France when the capitulation let it fall to the power of the English army'. So it was brought to London, where it was duly installed in the British Museum as the sarcophagus of Alexander the Great.

The error of identification was perhaps excusable. Although the multitude of texts covering the inside and outside walls of the sarcophagus were written in Egyptian

The Nile Delta

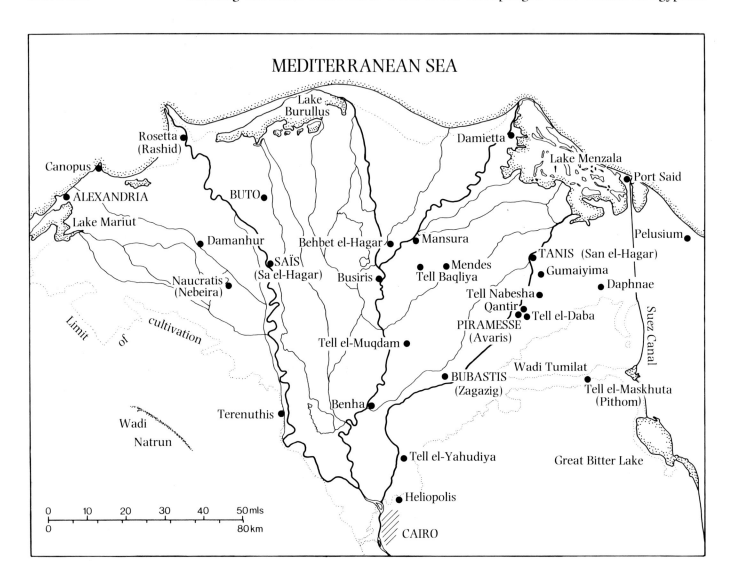

hieroglyphics, it was almost a fair assumption that if he had been buried after the custom of Egyptian Pharaohs, as tradition suggested, a coffin suitably inscribed in the Egyptian script would have held the mummified corpse. At least in one respect the modern identification was correct: it was a royal sarcophagus. It is not known where King Nectanebo had his tomb, but some indications point to the city of Isis (modern Behbet el-Hagar) in the middle Delta, where Nectanebo had built a fine temple to the goddess. The removal of the huge monument from the king's tomb to Alexandria could have happened at any time after the despoliation of the burial, even at the time of the foundation of the city by Alexander himself in 332 BC, or shortly afterwards. Its subsequent adaptation to a more humble purpose necessitated the boring of a series of twelve plug-holes around the base to allow the periodic draining of the coffin-chest, presumably whenever the water within became too rich a mixture.

Alexandria, never in antiquity a true Egyptian city, was well placed for sea-borne trade but singularly separated from the rest of the Delta by salt lakes and sandy wastes. Its indigenous antiquities were Graeco-Roman, but many of the pieces which fill the great museum in the city show Egyptian influence. At least one fine schist head of a young man, probably of the first century BC, indicates the direction in which classical portraiture was to travel in the early Roman imperial period, distinctly influenced by the strong Egyptian veristic tradition of the last dynasties.

The Greeks who ruled Egypt during the Ptolemaic Period imposed their own stamp on their adopted country, the most influential element of which was their language. Greek became the court language, the medium for the bureaucracy at its highest level, the speech of traders. It could not oust Egyptian among the bulk of the population, but it could be set above it in official pronouncements, and in important religious decrees it might appear in equal terms beside the hieroglyphic script. It was this last happy fact which caused Egyptian priests in 196 BC to commemorate the great benefits received by the land and temples of Egypt from King Ptolemy V Epiphanes, by erecting throughout Egypt inscriptions marking the event. The text of the decree promulgated on that occasion was published in Greek and Egyptian, two forms of the latter, the formal hieroglyphic and the cursive demotic, being used. Only one example of the triple decree has survived, in damaged state, and that was found at Rashid, a small town on the bleak coast about fifty awkward miles journey east of Alexandria, and now commonly known as Rosetta.

The terrifying unpredictability of chance played a formidable role in the discovery of the Rosetta Stone in 1799. During the Napoleonic occupation of Egypt, a detachment of the French army was stationed at Rashid, and in the course of the enlargement of a strong-point known as Fort Julien a large basalt slab was found, apparently built into a wall. The French engineer officer in charge, Pierre Bouchard, examining it and finding three separate bands of inscription, drew the imaginative conclusion that in these three bands might lie the key for the decipherment of the hieroglyphic script. A less interested and less informed officer might so easily have thought nothing of the stone and ordered it to be incorporated in the building of the fort, perhaps as the threshold to a doorway. So might the stone have passed back into oblivion and the efforts of the decipherers of the hieroglyphic script have been frustrated perhaps for many decades.

As it happened, the Institute already set up in the same year in Cairo by Napoleon's cadre of scholars was ready and waiting to exploit such a discovery. Bouchard passed the Rosetta Stone to his commander General Menou, who forwarded it to the Institute. The three bands of text – hieroglyphic, demotic and Greek – were subjected to close scrutiny; the Greek was quickly translated in a provisional manner; copies of the inscriptions were taken and sent to Europe. The French, however, were not to enjoy the full success of the discovery. In 1801, by the treaty of capitulation, after the defeat of Napoleon's forces, the Rosetta Stone, along with other antiquities collected by the French, was, like the sarcophagus of Nectanebo II, confiscated, taken to England and in due course placed in the British Museum. It was, it may be thought, a fair balancing of the fates which permitted the final decipherment of hieroglyphs to be effected by a French scholar, Jean-François Champollion.

Nowadays it seems incredible that the news of the discovery of the Rosetta Stone made such an impact on the minds of so many people. Even a British army officer could be moved to utter stirring sentiments about it. Major-General Tomkyns Hilgrove Turner singled out the piece for special conveyance to London and reported that the Secretary of State had 'acceded to my request, and permitted it to remain some time in the apartments of the Society of Antiquaries, previous to its deposition in the British Museum, where I trust it will long remain, a most valuable relic of antiquity, the feeble but only yet discovered link of the Egyptian to the known languages . . .'. And so it has remained,

6 The Rosetta Stone, carrying in three scripts the text of a priestly decree honouring Ptolemy V Epiphanes, dated to 196 BC.

7 (overleaf) A view over the temple area at Tanis, showing the remains of obelisks and colossal sculptures brought to the site from elsewhere by the kings of the Twenty-first Dynasty.

apart from one brief excursion to Paris in 1972 to take part in the celebrations marking the 150th anniversary of Champollion's announcement of the breakthrough which soon led to the understanding of the ancient Egyptian language. When the stone was unpacked from its crate in the Salle Henri IV at the Musée du Louvre, as much interest was directed towards the short inscription written on one side of the monument as to the three main texts themselves. In faded white letters, recognisably Georgian, could be read: CAPTURED IN EGYPT BY THE BRITISH ARMY 1801.

An archaeological assault was made on the Delta by the Egypt Exploration Fund (now Society) in the ten years after its foundation in 1882. The Fund had been founded expressly to reverse the process of destruction of the monuments of Egypt which had so shocked Miss Amelia B. Edwards, a well-known and successful Victorian novelist, who had visited Egypt in 1874. It was a time-consuming and frustrating task to secure adequate support from scholars and wealthy men of affairs for the launching of the Fund. To catch the interest of the general public was essential if it were to have a future. And so, in the very first public advertisement for the Fund, the organisers went straight for the nerve which would evoke a strong response from the god-fearing, intellectually curious British (and soon American) public. Announcing the new society this bait was dangled in front of prospective members:

It is proposed to raise a fund for the purpose of conducting excavations in the Delta . . . here most undoubtedly lie concealed the documents of a lost period of Biblical history – documents which we may confidently hope will furnish the key to a whole series of perplexing problems.

In 1883 the first season of excavation by the fledgling British society was carried out under the directorship of Edouard Naville, a Swiss Egyptologist with a strong interest in Biblical history. His attention was drawn to the Wadi Tumilat, a somewhat arid valley leading eastwards from the Delta towards the Suez Canal. Here might be found one of the cities mentioned in the Bible on the building of which the Israelites had laboured. Pithom and Raamses were the Biblical names, easily recognisable as the ancient Egyptian Per-Atum (House of the god Atum) and Per-Ramesse (House of the King Ramesses). The remains of one site, Tell el-Maskhuta, had been identified as Raamses and it was here that Naville dug. He convinced himself that the place was in fact Pithom and that the general area was the Land of Goshen where the Israelites settled on arrival in Egypt.

Naville was the kind of excavator who finds what he is looking for, working from the unknown to the known rather than from the known to the unknown. But his discoveries, from the historical point of view now largely discounted, were just what was needed to boost the membership of the Egypt Exploration Fund. He also brought back two pieces of sculpture, specially granted by the Egyptian Antiquities Service, the very first antiquities from legitimate modern excavation to come to Great Britain. They were presented by the Fund to the British Museum, thereby establishing the custom of presentation to the national museum which has continued down to the present time. One statue in red granite shows an official called Ankh-renp-nefer squatting on the ground, holding a shrine containing a figure of Atum. The subject, who carries a scarab-beetle on his head, held appointments during the Twenty-second Dynasty (c. 870 BC) in Pithom and other towns in the neighbourhood of the Wadi Tumilat; it helped to mislead Naville in his identification of the site. It is as if an inscribed bust of a mayor of Barnet, found in St Albans, were to persuade its discoverer that St Albans was in fact Barnet. The

8 Granite triad representing King Ramesses II seated between the gods Re and Atum. It is seen in position at Pithom in the late nineteenth century.

9 A roaring hippopotamus, denizen of the Delta swamps in antiquity. It is made of faience and is of Middle-Kingdom date.

second sculpture was of a falcon, an image of the sun-god Re-Herakhty, which carried in very bold hieroglyphs the name of King Ramesses II (1290–1224 BC), the very Pharaoh for whom the Biblical city of Raamses had been built.

The search for Raamses took another excavator of the Egypt Exploration Fund to a site about thirty-five miles to the north-west of Tell el-Maskhuta. The year was still 1883, but the excavator was a very different species of investigator, the legendary William Matthew Flinders Petrie. He was at the very outset of his long career in Egypt. He had surveyed the Pyramids of Giza in 1880–82, an apprenticeship in Egyptian archaeology which gave him the confidence at the age of 30 to take on, technically as a field archaeologist and intellectually as an Egyptologist, established scholars like Naville who saw him as a tiresome, interfering know-all and busy-body. Petrie never allowed a lack of formal training or an inadequacy of knowledge to stand in his way, but it must be admitted that in matters purely archaeological he could nearly always knock spots off his critics and opponents.

His choice of site for excavation was a vast mound which lay a little to the south of the land-locked lagoon of Lake Menzala in the north-east Delta. Today called San el-Hagar, it was anciently Tanis (to use the Greek form) and it had been partially excavated by Auguste Mariette twenty years before Petrie decided that it was the real site of Biblical Raamses. There was undoubtedly an element of perversity, if not of crude competition, in this redirection of effort to Tanis. But Petrie was not primarily interested in the possible Biblical associations of the place. He was after what he thought would be much more interesting historical results. The city founded by Ramesses II, Piramesse in Egyptian, was built on or near the site of the city of Avaris, the capital of the Hyksos, who were Asiatic settlers in Egypt during the first half of the second millennium BC. For a time during the years called the Second Intermediate Period (1786–1550 BC) they took control of the whole of the Delta and a large part of Upper Egypt. At one time they were

10 Nebamun takes his family fowling in the marshes, accompanied by a retriever cat.

commonly called the Shepherd Kings and were even identified with the Israelites in Egypt. Much mystery surrounded them, as it still does today, and Petrie hoped to solve some of the problems by working at Tanis.

In the event none of these problems were solved in the relatively short time spent by Petrie in this remote and desolate spot. He cleared and recorded the vast temple area and excavated houses in the town-mound dating from the Graeco-Roman Period. Many additional puzzles were created by conflicting evidence, especially by the presence of royal sculptures of many periods, some going back to the Middle Kingdom but most dating from the time of Ramesses II. It seemed certain that Tanis was Piramesse, and therefore, presumably, Avaris, but no trace could be found of domestic remains of either the Nineteenth Dynasty or the Hyksos.

Yet, like Naville, Petrie was sure that he had found what he was looking for, and his identification of Tanis with Piramesse/Avaris prevailed until after the Second World War. In short, Piramesse is almost without a doubt to be placed at Qantir, about fifteen miles south of Tanis, where the remains of royal palaces and associated buildings have been found; while Avaris was located at Tell el-Daba, a site which in antiquity probably lay within the broad boundaries of Piramesse. Exemplary modern investigations by Austrian and Egyptian archaeologists have, it seems, settled that problem.

It is extraordinary to contemplate what happened between about 1300 BC and 1000 BC in this apparent backwater of modern Egypt. During the early years of the Nineteenth Dynasty a royal summer palace was built in or near Avaris and here the new city of Piramesse was established soon after the accession of Ramesses II. Huge quantities of sculptures from earlier periods were shipped down river to provide the new city with imposing monuments, and most of these were 'modified' by having Ramesses' names added. Towards the end of the Twentieth Dynasty (c. 1080 BC) the branch of the Nile on which Piramesse stood began to silt up and ceased to be a practicable waterway. Then Tanis, for political as well as practical reasons became the most important Delta city, and the kings of the Twenty-first and Twenty-second Dynasties again shifted the sculptures of Piramesse to Tanis. So, monuments of many earlier periods graced the new royal city of Tanis, and in modern times greatly confused those scholars who sought simple solutions from very misleading evidence.

In its day Piramesse must have been a wonderful place, that is if we may believe the extravagant descriptions contained in a number of papyri belonging to a group which contain well-composed but difficult short essays, full of unusual words, designed, it is thought, to train young scribes in writing down accurate versions from dictation. Piramesse gave scope for hyperbole:

His Majesty (may he live, be prosperous and healthy) has constructed a palace named 'Great-of-Victories'. It lies between Syria and Egypt proper and is stocked with food and provisions. It is planned like Thebes in Upper Egypt, and its continuation is like Memphis. The sun rises and sets within its horizon. All have deserted their own towns and come to live in its neighbourhood. Its west is the Temple of Amun, its south is the Temple of Seth; in its east is Astarte, and in its northern region Edjo [a cobra-goddess].

More detail is provided by another passage. A scribe purports to write:

I have arrived in Piramesse – beloved of Amun (may he live, be prosperous and healthy) and have found it to be in excellent condition: a splendid district without equal, laid out like Thebes. Re founded it himself. The residence is pleasant to live in; its fields are full of all good things. There are fishes in its ponds, and birds in its pools. Its meadows are green with pasture . . . Its granaries are full of barley and emmer-wheat . . . onions and leeks . . . lettuce . . . pomegranates, apples and olives, figs of the orchard and smooth wine of Ka-en-keme [a famous Delta vineyard] better than honey . . . [a very extensive catalogue of available fish intervenes with various other matters of eulogy] . . . Its boats proceed and moor. Food and provisions are there every day. Joy inhabits it, and nobody says: "If only . . . !" Small people in it are like great people. Come, let us celebrate its festivals of heaven and its feasts month by month . . . The young people of 'Great-of-Victories' are dressed for festival every day with sweet oil on their heads and their hair newly curled . . . Live and be happy, and walk freely about without needing to move from there.

From the time of the Old Kingdom the Delta was a place for resort, for getting away from metropolitan life, for a return to a simpler form of existence. Evidence from tombs shows that important people owned estates there, and that the relatively untamed terrain in many parts was ideal country for field sports. The very tradition of the great man spearing fish and hunting birds in the papyrus thickets and marshes has its proper earthly location in the Delta. But if you contemplate the exceptionally fine Theban tomb-painting of Nebamun fowling in the marshes, you can hardly fail to wonder what truth lies behind the representation. Nebamun himself is lightly dressed and stands poised to hurl his throw-stick; his wife, on the other hand, wears what is probably her best gown, clasps an elaborate bouquet and sports lotus-flowers and a cone of scented ointment on her head. Their young daughter squats between Nebamun's legs, plucking a lotus-flower from the water; she is nude but for an elaborate floral collar and lotus pendant. In this depiction of a standard scene there is much to admire, but it is totally idealised. No family party ever went fowling in this manner. Yet it still preserves the memory of hunting in the Delta marshes, an environment scarcely seen but vividly invoked by the master-painter of Nebamun's tomb.

Of the many sites throughout the Delta examined by Petrie and Naville, few yielded such fine and interesting pieces as Bubastis, a royal city in the Twenty-second Dynasty and the recipient of sculpture and monumental stonework from Piramesse (but to a lesser extent than Tanis). Bubastis, however, had had a long and distinguished career as a provincial capital and cult-centre before it achieved the royal accolade. It was above all the sacred base for the cat-goddess Bastet, 'the House of Bastet', just as the earlier royal residence was Piramesse (Per-Ramesse), 'the House of Ramesses'; from Per-Bastet comes the Greek name Bubastis.

The prominence given to Bubastis by the kings of the Twenty-second Dynasty, especially Osorkon II (c. 883–855 BC), derived from their local family attachments; but the continued importance of the city in later times derived from the great sanctuary of Bastet. The Greeks, quaintly, equated this goddess with their own Artemis, and Herodotus, the Greek historian, who visited Egypt in the fifth century BC, puts the annual festival of 'Artemis' at Bubastis at the head of all the great Egyptian religious gatherings. He describes how crowds of men, women and children descend on Bubastis, mostly by boat, just as unruly, drunk and foul-mouthed as the away football crowd of popular imagination. As the boats pass along the waterways ribald songs are sung, accompanied by flutes and rhythmic hand-clapping; vulgarities are shouted at villagers who make the mistake of watching the procession go by, and women stand up and expose their

**11** Bronze figure of the cat sacred to the goddess Bastet. A silver pectoral with the sacred eye of Horus decorates its chest.

**12** The remains of the city mound at Bubastis in 1963.

attractions in a blatantly provocative manner. Herodotus reported that over 700,000 people would attend this festival and that more grape-wine was drunk in its course than in the whole of the rest of the year put together.

Herodotus was inclined to accept a good story rather uncritically. Yet there is no reason to doubt that the periodic festivals in Bubastis were well attended. It may have been on such occasions that huge numbers of mummified cats were offered to the deity. Extensive cat cemeteries were laid out not far from the great temple and from these have come many of the cat-mummies and bronze cats which are found in most Egyptian collections. Among the divine images of Bastet are some which show her as a woman with cat-head, wearing what seems to be a loosely knitted but clinging long dress, and carrying what has been described as her 'shopping-basket'. Kittens sometimes tumble about her feet, emphasising the benevolent aspects of this feline deity who can, however, assume rather more severe characteristics when she is associated with the lioness Sakhmet at Memphis.

To visit Bubastis now with expectations based on Herodotus' account is a dispiriting experience. From Cairo you travel to the delightfully named Zagazig, a place transformed in recent years by industry and a huge growth in population. The modern town, with its only too evident factories, hedges in the ancient site; the steady spread of habitation trespasses on the pitiful remains of the ancient metropolis. The main *tell* or mound of Bubastis rises only a few metres above the surrounding land, and the remains of the great temple lie about in tumbled confusion. Apart from the threatening encroachments of modern Zagazig, Bubastis was much the same when Edouard Naville arrived there in 1887. Then the temple remains were extensively buried under heaps of decayed domestic buildings of later periods, and Naville had great difficulty in exposing the ancient granite ruins. He found a temple which had been almost totally destroyed, undoubtedly in antiquity, possibly by an earthquake. To make sense of the site he had to unpick the tangled mass of blocks, spreading them out and rolling them over to reveal their carved scenes and inscriptions. On paper, reconstruction of parts of the great religious complex could give some idea of the magnificence of the main temple and especially of its great Jubilee Portal. But, in Naville's estimation, only about one-third of the original building had survived to modern times. The bulk of its decoration was carried out in the Twenty-second Dynasty, but, as Petrie had found at Tanis, statues, monuments and inscriptions bearing names of earlier kings, here going as far back as King Cheops of the Fourth Dynasty (c. 2551–2528 BC, the builder of the Great Pyramid), made the historical interpretation of the site exceptionally hazardous. Many of the problems remain to be solved.

From the artistic point of view one of the finest Bubastite sculptures is a fragmentary granite colossus from the entrance to the great hall of the temple. Much of it is missing; the great base, showing the lower part of a seated king, partially survives in three pieces, but the head, happily, is almost intact. As a whole this statue encapsulates many of the contradictory elements which confused not only the early excavators of the Delta sites, but also later Egyptologists. The readable cartouches on the base identify the represented king as Osorkon II, the principal architect of Bubastis' glory. But there are clear signs that the cartouches contain altered names. Who then was the monarch for whom the statue was made? Naville and others at the time of discovery saw in the features of the head

11

13

13 Granite head of King Ammenemes III from a seated colossus usurped by King Osorkon II for his temple at Bubastis.

**14** Glazed tile from the decorative scheme used probably in the throne room of the palace of King Ramesses III at Tell el-Yahudiya. It shows a bound Libyan captive.

**15** Granite relief from the temple at Bubastis, showing King Osorkon II with his wife Karoma paying homage to an unidentified deity.

lineaments which suggested an Asiatic type; it was then only a short step to identify the original as one of the Hyksos, the Shepherd Kings, and an even shorter one to name him as Apophis or Apepi, as he was then called. This identification, however, was soon reappraised. Here – and agreement among scholars has been overwhelmingly consistent – is a representation of King Ammenemes III of the Twelfth Dynasty (c. 1844–1797 BC); not just a routine example of standard royal portraiture, but a true masterpiece. The typical physiognomy of the king, full-faced with distinctively high and prominent cheekbones, is superbly carved in monumental size – strong and yet exceptionally sensitive. The colossus is, it seems, a piece of the Twelfth Dynasty usurped by a king of the Twenty-second Dynasty, almost one thousand years later. Archaeological studies in recent years have demonstrated that many other usurped pieces at Bubastis must have been brought there, probably by Osorkon II, to furnish the great new temple with ready-made sculptures. There is good reason to think that this Ammenemes may have first been placed in Memphis. But did it travel straight to Bubastis, or by way of Piramesse, having first been hi-jacked by Ramesses II?

Similar questions can be aimed at other sculptures and monumental pieces from Bubastis. The upper part of a red granite colossus of Ramesses II is one of four similar sculptures which almost certainly came from Piramesse; and the same is probably true of a granite column over twenty feet high with the names of Ramesses II partly expunged and replaced by those of Osorkon II. It is hard to contemplate the wholesale shifting about of huge monuments up and down the waterways of the Delta in ancient times – the inescapable consequence of wishing to build mighty buildings embellished with sculptures out of stones the nearest quarries for which lay many hundreds of miles upstream at Aswan. Why not pillage the work of a predecessor in a place near by, and make his temple the quarry? No doubt he had done the same for his own new temple. One of the less admirable characteristics of ancient Egyptian kings was their inability to respect the works of their ancestors, except in very particular cases.

Of several Bubastite reliefs which truly date from the reign of Osorkon II and which may therefore be absolved of the stigma of being 'second-hand', the finest shows Osorkon, followed by his wife Karoma, worshipping a deity. The sunk relief, carved with exemplary precision and, in the case of Karoma, a very satisfactory voluptuousness, shows how excellently the skills of Egyptian artist-masons had survived into a period which is generally not notable for good sculpture.

The extent of excavation in Delta sites in the late nineteenth century seems, from the perspective of today's activities in Egypt, not only heroic but also quite remarkably far-seeing. Over twenty important places were investigated to a greater or lesser degree, some like Bubastis over several seasons, others, like Mendes, Tell el-Muqdam and Tell Baqliya by rapid survey. Major monuments were not always found, or, if found, brought out of Egypt. Nevertheless, the urgent methods used, especially by Flinders Petrie, frequently discovered important historical facts, and produced tangible results in the form of large numbers of small objects. These provided the raw material for a reappraisal of Egyptian culture which had previously been judged chiefly on the basis of the archaeological discoveries and standing monuments in the Nile Valley south of Cairo. Some of the most interesting Delta finds concerned the manufacturing processes employed by the Egyptians in antiquity. Petrie, in particular, was fascinated by things technical and had a genius for finding the remains of workshops and industrial sites – not all of them deserving quite the description of 'factory' which he was inclined to give them. Fine discoveries of glass were made at Gumaiyima, including much evidence of glass-workings. At Tell el-Yahudiya ('The Mound of the Jew'), unusual structures, probably built by the Hyksos, were uncovered, and in the area of the temple and palace of the Nineteenth and Twentieth Dynasties more of the elaborately glazed decorative tiles of 14 which large numbers had been found earlier in the nineteenth century.

At Nebeira in the Western Delta Petrie again found traces of industrial processes for the making of a quite distinctive kind of faience, or glazed quartz frit, used for scarabs, small figurines and decorative elements. But more importantly he was able to identify at Nebeira the site of the ancient city of Naucratis, which in the reign of Amasis in the Twenty-sixth Dynasty (570–526 BC) had been granted a monopoly for Greek trading in Egypt. Petrie described how on his first visit he found that he could not walk over the site without crunching sherds of Greek vases under his feet: 'It seemed as if I was wandering 16 in the smashings of the Museum's vase-room'. The main town-mound had already been disastrously reduced by the removal of decayed mud-brick for fertilisers by local farmers; the sherds had been left behind in thick profusion, a sad testimony of what might have been found in a rather better state of preservation had the mound been left untouched.

In considering the greatly diminished remains of Naucratis, Petrie conceded that his task in excavation was made much easier by the absence of a huge *tell* as at Tanis. But he

16 A bowl of East Greek manufacture from Naucratis (*c*. 600–500 BC), decorated with female heads on the rim, and friezes of boars, lions, sphinxes, goats and geese. The Greek inscription reads: 'Sostratos dedicated me to Aphrodite'.

also recognised the desperate necessity for rapid investigation before all traces were gone. What he and his successor Ernest Gardner were able to recover from the site in two seasons proved to be an immensely valuable, if disappointingly modest, record of what had been the most important Greek city in Egypt before the foundation of Alexandria.

In a lecture delivered to the Egypt Exploration Fund on 28 October 1885 Petrie reflected:

A generation back there stood in the green plain of the Delta, about halfway between Cairo and Alexandria, a mound of dust with the past of Naukratis entombed within it. Today all the heart of it is gone, spread out on the fields of the country . . . and the antiquities which it contained cast forth without a name or history among the collections of the world, if their intrinsic worth prevented their immediate destruction. 'Where was Naukratis?' the geographer and historian were asking, while every year saw hundreds of visitors to Egypt passing within two or three miles of the fast vanishing ruins of that city.

His lament for Naucratis, urgent a century ago, remains as vitally pertinent today as the twentieth century draws to a close. Fewer travellers than ever pass within a few miles of Naucratis, apart from those who may use the road to Alexandria from Cairo through the cultivation. American archaeologists have worked on this site in recent years, and to that extent Naucratis is less neglected than most ancient towns in the Delta. But the region as a whole deserves better treatment; it should become the scene for intensive rescue excavation before even more ancient mounds are spread thin over their neighbouring fields. The Delta must cease to be the forgotten land; it should be worked in, visited by tourists, thought about and written about. Much of Egypt's most ancient past remains to be revealed through its exploration.

# CHAPTER TWO
# Metropolis and Necropolis
## MEMPHIS AND ITS CEMETERIES

THE WRITER of one of the 'essays' in the document known as Papyrus Anastasi IV in the British Museum speaks of his great nostalgia for the city of Memphis:

See! my heart has stolen forth and goes quietly to a place that it knows well. It has gone downstream to see Hikuptah [Memphis]. Would that I could sit quietly, waiting for my heart to tell me how things are in Men-nefer [Memphis]! But my hand can accomplish nothing while my heart is away from its proper place. Come to me, Ptah, and take me to Men-nefer. Let me see you without difficulty.

Here, apparently – for the circumstances of the composition are quite unclear – the writer longs to be in Memphis, to know what is happening there and to see Ptah, the city's great god. He calls the city Men-nefer and Hikuptah: the former, an abbreviation of Pepi-men-nefer, the name given to the pyramid and settlement established by King Pepi I of the Sixth Dynasty (*c.* 2289–2255 BC), at nearby Saqqara; the latter a name meaning 'the mansion of the *Ka* (spirit) of Ptah', from which in later times came the Greek name Aigyptos and, in turn, our present Egypt.

The passionate encomium of a particular place and its god is not uncommon in Egyptian literature, and too much attention should not, perhaps, be paid to this specific

**18** Part of the Ptah temple complex at Memphis.

19 Granite statue of the ship-builder Ankhwa.

literary outburst on behalf of Memphis. But who now can say much in favour of the city as a place to long for? Its site, a few miles upstream from Cairo, to the west of the modern course of the Nile, is as much a wreck as many of the eroded mounds of the Delta cities. It is, however, rather more picturesque, for its mounds, many of which are still occupied by busy villages, lie within lush palm groves and bustle with village life. Here is an archaeologist's nightmare and, at the same time, his most tempting challenge, a place of the greatest importance in antiquity, encumbered by the barnacles of modern occupation yet almost untouched by the scholar's spade.

Very little of Memphis's great past can be seen by the present-day visitor, who may be brought to what is now called Mit Rahina for a brief visit before the real treats of the day may be enjoyed up on the desert scarp at Saqqara. He will see the great alabaster colossus of Ramesses II lying prone in its inelegant, but functional, concrete shelter; he may walk among the few monumental remains gathered together in the adjacent small outdoor museum which is dominated by an alabaster sphinx of uncertain date. After a brush or two with the licensed 'antique'-dealers whose booths provide variety among the almost meaningless monuments (unlabelled and divorced from their original settings) the visitor will board his bus and be swept away in a swirl of dust and small boys. He will not have seen the sad remains of the great temple of Ptah, or the interesting site which may – or may not, if recent researches are confirmed – be the place where the great Apis bulls were embalmed and prepared for the long funeral haul to their sacred catacomb at Saqqara. He will not have been encouraged to wander among the palm trees, to wonder what extraordinary buildings are signalled by the brick outcrops and decayed limestone fragments which break the surfaces of the dusty hillocks stretching into the distance in all directions.

It needs little imagination to appreciate the huge area which still represents the visible site of ancient Memphis, about two miles from north to south and one mile from east to west; but what can now be identified as the remains of an ancient occupied site represents only a small part – perhaps the core – of the city when it achieved its greatest extent, probably in the Ptolemaic-Roman Period. Flinders Petrie, who worked in Memphis first in 1908, estimated the full extent of the ancient city at about eight miles from north to south and four miles from east to west, basing his calculations on figures given by Diodorus Siculus, a well-known purveyor of borrowed information. Petrie allowed that much of the huge areas so enclosed would consist of 'gardens and fields belonging to the various villages, which were agglomerated to form the capital, like the component villages and towns of London.' He reckoned that its size could be compared with northern London 'from Bow to Chelsea, and from the Thames up to Hampstead'.

There is probably more truth in Petrie's comparison than in Diodorus' fanciful figures. Memphis was huge by ancient standards and its size and regular growth throughout the Pharaonic age down to the Graeco-Roman Period resulted from its continuously dominant position politically, bureaucratically and commercially throughout the three thousand years of Egyptian antiquity. And this estimate makes no allowance for the immense importance of Memphis as a religious centre. It is perhaps ironic that what evidence survives today as the visible testimony of past Memphite greatness is almost wholly religious. Happily there are many other indications, less apparent to the casual observer, which provide the corrective. Much can be learned from the tombs of the great

Memphite officials, especially those who exercised their various functions during the New Kingdom and later, and who were buried at Saqqara. And there are a few documents written on papyri, which shed light, sometimes intensely, on moments of time and corners of space, when and where Memphis is concerned.

Menes, the first king of the First Dynasty, (*c.* 2920 BC), the legendary unifier of Upper and Lower Egypt, founded the first capital to serve the whole country at Memphis. At first, called White Walls, it was essentially the royal palace, itself the political centre of the country. With its foundation came the first use of the desert plateau to the west as the Memphite burial ground. Saqqara saw the first great tombs and also the first great stone building, the Step Pyramid of King Djoser of the Third Dynasty (*c.* 2630–2611 BC), the limestone enclosure wall of which probably reproduced, in a more enduring material than that of its inspiration, the White Walls of Menes' palace in the city of Memphis.

19 From this time dates one of the earliest complete statues, which represents a boat-builder who used to be called Bedjmes. Now, after a reappraisal of the difficult inscription on the lap above the left knee, Ankhwa seems more properly to be the name, while Bedjmes is possibly that of his father. The statue, carved in red granite, shows Ankhwa seated on a block seat with an adze – the characteristic tool of the boat-builder – slung over his left shoulder. It possesses the chunky, squat style of Early Dynastic sculpture, carved economically but with great mastery of a hard, unyielding medium; bodily contours are subtly suggested and the head and wig strongly rendered. Not the least interesting thing

20 The necropolis plateau of Saqqara with the Step Pyramid, viewed from the city remains of Memphis.

21 Bronze figure of Isis nursing Horus. The gold mask covering the goddess's face is of substantial thickness; the wooden base is original.

22 Bronze group of a king making an offering to the Apis bull; a dedication of a man named Peftjawemawyhor.

*Opposite:* Memphis and its necropolis area.

23 *(overleaf)* The Great Sphinx at Giza.

about this powerful piece is the social background it suggests, in which a senior craftsman working almost certainly in the Memphite region, but with no apparent royal connection beyond the commonplace title 'he who is concerned with the affairs of the king' (perhaps, even at this early date to be rendered, less specifically, but more suggestively, 'king's acquaintance'), was able to provide himself with such an impressive statue, presumably for his tomb.

Stone clearly came into its own during the Third Dynasty, but in its use the Egyptians were in a sense very selective. The distinction in building between the use of mud-brick and stone was not simply one of convenience. The difference is explained simply in the contemplation of the palace and the pyramid and their essential materials: brick for the palace, stone for the tomb – the one ephemeral, the other enduring. This contrast has already been met in the Delta, and it will be met again constantly throughout this journey through Egypt. Brick was nearly always used for ancient Egyptian buildings other than tombs and temples, as it still is today in most villages. And in the ancient towns throughout Egypt, usually sited on slight eminences above the annual flood-waters, brick returned to earth as homes crumbled and were replaced, were built over and in time were submerged below the ever-rising water-level. Stone buildings, if they were placed well above the limits of the Nile's inundation, were almost eternal (as tombs and temples were considered to be), unless they were deliberately destroyed, quarried, or tumbled by earthquake. A stone building sited in a town slowly sank, as it seems, while the land around it rose higher and higher with each year's deposition of mud by the inundation.

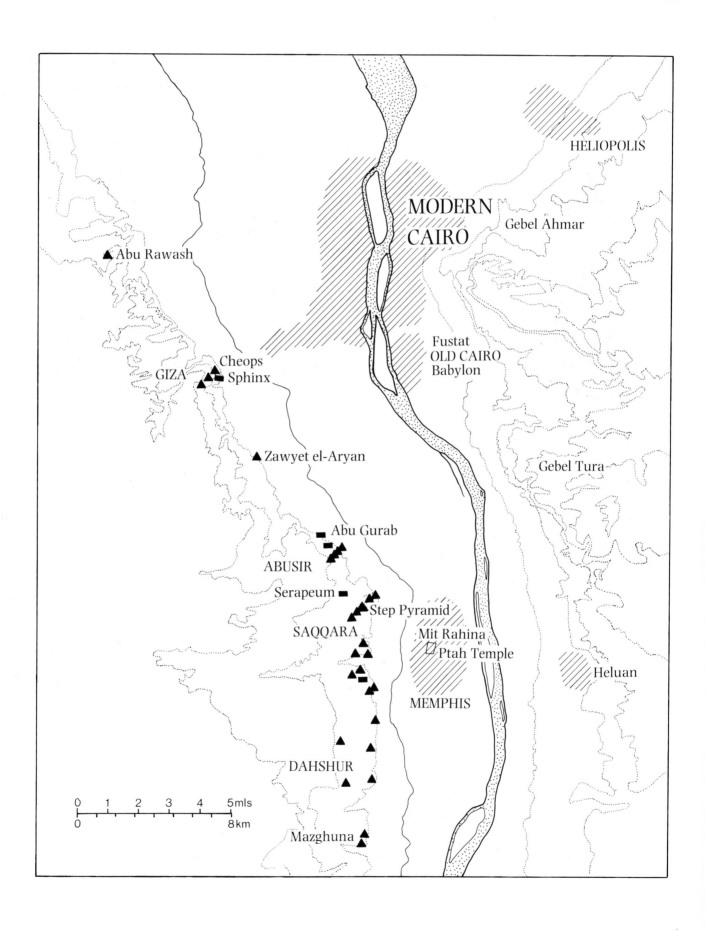

HELIOPOLIS

MODERN
CAIRO

Gebel Ahmar

▲ Abu Rawash

Fustat
OLD CAIRO
Babylon

Cheops
GIZA ▲▲ Sphinx

Gebel Tura

▲ Zawyet el-Aryan

▬ Abu Gurab
▬▲▲
ABUSIR ▲▲

Serapeum ▬
▲▲ Step Pyramid
SAQQARA

Mit Rahina
Ptah Temple
▲▲▲
Heluan
▲▬
▲ MEMPHIS

▲

▲
▲

DAHSHUR
▲ ▲

0   1   2   3   4   5mls
0                   8km

Mazghuna ▲▲

It is therefore not surprising that temples and tombs, and especially the latter, have always been seen by excavators in Egypt as the easy option. The tombs of the Memphite necropolis have traditionally provided the easiest point of reference and source of antiquities for the dealers of Cairo and, in the past, for the traveller on the look-out for a worthy souvenir of a memorable visit to Egypt. After the initial exploitation of Saqqara up to the Third Dynasty, the area of possible interment was massively extended over nearly twenty miles from Dahshur in the south to Abu Rawash in the north, without mentioning Maidum yet further to the south, which will be included in the next chapter. These twenty miles encompass the great Giza pyramid plateau, developed by the kings of the Fourth Dynasty for their own burials and for those of their families, nobles and officials, who populated the Memphite court; then, between Giza and Saqqara, were Abu Gurab and Abusir, where the kings of the Fifth Dynasty built sun-temples and pyramids. But Saqqara was continuously the most important burial ground, with tombs of almost all ages right down to the Graeco-Roman Period, their number and quality reflecting quite conclusively the varying fortunes of Memphis from period to period. To cap its history in a remarkable manner, Saqqara at the last became a place of pilgrimage on an extraordinary scale – a kind of religious state fair on a permanent site, where shrines to all the Memphite deities, and many others besides, jostled one another among and over the burials of earlier periods.

First among the great shrines was the temple attached to the huge catacomb where the mummified Apis bulls were laid to rest, each in his individual stone coffin, filed away neatly in its own massive niche. The Serapeum, as the catacomb is now called, is a misnomer; if applied to anything, the name more properly fits the temple which was dedicated to the dual deity Osiris-Apis, the embodiment of the sacred Apis bull in death. Serapis, the deity 'invented' in the Ptolemaic Period to act as link between the religions of Egypt and the Greeks in Egypt, undoubtedly derived his name from Osiris-Apis. However, in form he was no bull-god, but a bearded Zeus-like divinity with funerary aspects. Apis himself, a divine symbol of power and fertility closely associated with Ptah, the great god of Memphis, was manifested in a bull calf with special markings, maintained throughout its life in special quarters in the Ptah precinct at Memphis, and buried with full, royal pomp when it died. In one respect Apis symbolised the power of the king, and his cult was always one specially promoted by the king. The relationship is made clear in a bronze group showing an unidentified king kneeling in the act of presenting some offering before the Apis bull. The inscription on the base of the bull shows that the dedicator of the group was a man named Peftjawemawyhor, who probably lived and made his dedication in the Twenty-sixth Dynasty (*c.* 600 BC).

Much has been learned in recent years about the circumstances of dedication, and the fate of dedicated objects, from excavations carried out in the northern part of Saqqara by the Egypt Exploration Society. This part of the great necropolis lay close to the ancient way leading from the Serapeum northwards down from the desert plateau in the direction of the modern village of Abusir and past the lake where the sacred ibises may have been reared. Here was discovered a temple of the Thirtieth Dynasty (*c.* 360 BC), possibly of earlier foundation, dedicated principally to the cults of Apis and of the Mothers of Apis, the physical cow-mothers of the Apis bulls, here identified with the goddess Isis. Close by were found catacombs not only of Mother of Apis burials but also of

24 The false door of
Ptahshepses from his Saqqara
tomb.

falcons, the living form of Horus, of baboons and of ibises (both living manifestations of the moon-god Thoth). Elsewhere at Saqqara, but not very far from this northern point, burials of cats (Bastet) and dogs (Anubis) had been found and plundered during the nineteenth century. In and around the temple terrace many caches of divine figures, amulets and larger sculptures were brought to light, as well as many papyri and ostraca (inscribed flakes of limestone and pottery sherds). Here in context were large numbers of bronze figures bearing dedications to the various deities whose cults were practised on the Saqqara plateau towards the end of the Pharaonic Period. What had been found in many cases probably represented the deliberate rejects from the various shrines – removed and buried because they crowded the space available for newly dedicated pieces, but yet sufficiently holy to be spared from destruction.

Many of the bronzes were carefully wrapped in linen and were in almost mint condition; others were so badly covered with corrosion that detail could not be seen. One figure of the goddess Isis nursing the child-god Horus was at the time of its discovery heavy with copper salt accretions, but a touch of gold could be seen embedded in the corrosion. When the bronze was fully cleaned it was found that the face of the goddess was covered with a tiny mask of thin sheet gold, robust enough to be removed and replaced without buckling – a remarkable survival from the hazards of its past. Another remarkable survival from among the temple discards is a wooden statue of an unnamed priestly official holding in front of his body an effigy of the god Ptah, shown, as was common, in the form of a mummiform image with head and face uncovered. Its survival is remarkable because in this part of the Saqqara necropolis most wood which escaped destruction by damp (it rains infrequently during the winter in this part of Egypt) has usually been consumed by termites. The statue as a whole can be dated to the late New Kingdom or a little later (c. 1100–900 BC), a period from which very little wooden sculpture from any site in Egypt has survived.

Although at the end of the Dynastic Period and in Graeco-Roman times Saqqara was a bustling place throughout the year with constant pilgrimages to the many shrines, where troubled souls sought comfort from the mysteries and incubation treatments available especially at the shrine of Thoth (known to the Greeks as Hermes), with regular festivals and processions and very occasionally an Apis funeral as special entertainment, the district was also probably rather run down suffering from the excessive usage of

21

almost three thousand years. To some extent its bustle reflected the busy life of the city of Memphis, which remained the most important centre of commerce and administration until it was superseded by Alexandria. It was a huge, amorphous, rambling place, with large 'ghettoes' made over for foreign communities – for Greeks, for Jews, for Carians, for Phoenicians. Apart from its temples it probably had few imposing buildings, and was mostly made up of warren-like districts of narrow streets and three-storey houses where collapse and rebuilding went on continuously: unsanitary, smelly, dusty or muddy according to the season, but full of life and interest. As the northern capital of Egypt it had always been important, particularly during the Eighteenth and Nineteenth Dynasties (c. 1550–1196 BC) when Egypt practised an active foreign policy to the east, and especially during the Old Kingdom when the great pyramid-building kings administered their kingdom centrally and positively from White Walls. Of Old Kingdom Memphis nothing survives; of New Kingdom Memphis there are many religious remains but as yet little else to illuminate the secular side of its life. New excavations by the Egypt Exploration Society may in time fill in some of the picture.

For Old Kingdom testimonies, however, one should visit the Memphite necropolis, which provides ample material for the historian and for the tourist. Who can easily forget the massiveness of the Giza pyramids, the mysterious power of the Sphinx, the majesty of the Step Pyramid and its dependent buildings, the exquisite low-relief scenes of Ty's *mastaba*-chapel, or the impressive scale of the Dahshur pyramids, especially the one called Bent? The reality of these extraordinary monuments can scarcely be matched by what a museum can show from the same places. Nevertheless, in several museums in Europe and the U.S.A. there are granite columns, nearly 19 feet high, which come from the funerary temple attached to the pyramid of King Unas of the Fifth Dynasty (c. 2356–2323 BC). They are monolithic, with capitals in the form of palm fronds; even out of context they still make a distinct impact on visitors who choose quietly to consider their meticulous manufacture and transport from quarry to temple (about 500 miles) rather more than 4,300 years ago.

Many inscriptions, scenes and parts of scenes come from the limestone *mastaba*-chapels of Giza and Saqqara. (*Mastaba* was the Arabic word, meaning 'bench', used by the Egyptian workmen employed in the mid-nineteenth century by Auguste Mariette, the founder of the Antiquities Service in Egypt, when he unearthed in primitive excavations large numbers of Old Kingdom tombs at Saqqara.) The tombs, generally speaking, consisted of a burial chamber at the bottom of a deep shaft, and a chapel housed in a rectangular structure on the surface above it. The sides of these superstructures sloped slightly and gave the general impression of benches. When even larger numbers of Old Kingdom tombs were excavated around the pyramids of Giza in the early decades of the twentieth century, the use of the word became even more apposite. At Giza the tombs were laid out in regular rows with their superstructures marshalled like the box-like dwellings of a modern housing estate. A mean regularity was imposed on the great who had served the king in life and were regimented in death in cramped sepulchres beneath closely ranked *mastaba*-chapels.

The surviving parts of the decorated walls of the chapel of Urirenptah give some idea of the functions of the chapel and its decorations, and of the variety of the latter. Urirenptah was a priestly official attached to the sun-temple of King Neferirkare of the Fifth Dynasty (*c.* 2446–2426 BC), whose pyramid is at Abusir, a few miles to the north of Saqqara, but whose sun-temple has never been identified. It was probably a little further to the north, at Abu Gurab, where Urirenptah carried out his duties, but his tomb was prepared in the principal burial ground of the Fifth and Sixth Dynasties at Saqqara. Offerings of food and drink were required for the regular sustenance of the spirit of the dead person and these were presented daily – if the system was operating according to plan – on offering slabs in the chapel before a niche arranged like a blind doorway and called, not surprisingly, the 'false door'. The principal wall of Urirenptah's chapel, opposite the entrance-door, contains two false doors, one for the use of the tomb-owner's spirit and the other for that of his wife, Khentkaus. The central panel of the principal false door, which in most other

25 Limestone pair statue of a high official and his wife, probably from a late Eighteenth-Dynasty tomb at Saqqara. It is uninscribed and therefore without identity.

26 Katep and his wife Hetepheres face eternity side by side. The reddish-brown and yellow with which they are painted are the conventional colours for male and female respectively.

47

cases is marked simply as if it were a door with a pair of simulated wooden door-valves and a door-bolt, is here marked out with an extensive 'menu' of ninety-six items which were to nourish the mind and body of Urirenptah in his afterlife. In the scenes which flank the false doors, the tomb-owner and his wife sit together – in one case Khentkaus squats on the floor – receiving the lavish presentation of offerings; bulls are slaughtered and dismembered; musicians play to entertain the guests at the eternal feast, and ladies dance a singularly stiff measure.

A second reasonably well-preserved wall carries a series of scenes in which Urirenptah sets forth to observe the activities in his fields, for he was, or at least chose to show himself as, a great landowner. His principal task is to inspect his accounts; scribes bring their documents and bailiffs drag along men who presumably have failed to pay up what they owe. Herds of donkeys and sheep are driven forward for inspection, and simultaneously (but in fact in chronological sequence) men sow grain, sheep tread the grain into the ground, flax and barley are harvested and huge bales of produce are carried from the fields by patient donkeys (the ancestors, surely, of those that work in the fields below the Saqqara plateau today). Slightly incongruously, but with admirable economy of space, a scene in which the master's bed is prepared is tucked in to the left of the harvest scene; lengths of bed-linen are taken from a chest by two servants while two more make up the bed and place a pillow head-rest in position.

The tomb chapel provided the visual environment in which the tomb-owner would pass eternity, fully provisioned and surrounded by activities with which he was well acquainted from his life on earth. Occasionally a corner of the veil of bland conformity and uninformative conventionality may be twitched to give a brief glimpse of something more of the life of the owner. Such is the case with the large and fine false door from the Saqqara *mastaba*-chapel of Ptahshepses who, as well as having priestly functions in most of the sun-temples of the kings of the Fifth Dynasty, also bore the title 'chief of the directors of craftsmen', showing that he was high-priest of Ptah in Memphis. A massive lintel, 13 feet 6 inches long, mounted above the false door is very finely carved with deeply cut hieroglyphs conveying the conventional invocations of the gods Osiris and Anubis. The false door itself is of unusual form, the door proper in the centre being flanked by panelled walls, the vertical panels, or pilasters of which carry snatches of what can only be described as an autobiographical text. Unfortunately the loss of blocks at the top of the panelled walls prevents a full understanding of Ptahshepses' notable career. The account is laconic in the extreme, one vertical line generally being allotted to his career during one reign. His life starts to unfold in the right-hand column, which tells how he was brought up among the royal children of King Mycerinus of the Fourth Dynasty (c. 2490–2472 BC); his education continued in royal circles in the reign of Shepseskaf; he married the princess Kha-ma'at, eldest daughter of either Shepseskaf or Userkaf, the first king of the Fifth Dynasty. Five further columns commemorate the honourable way in which he was treated by successive kings down at least to Nyuserre in the late Fifth Dynasty (c. 2416–2392 BC). It is even possible that he lived on into the reigns of Menkauhor and Djedkare-Isesi, but sadly the royal names are lost. To pretend that this text is a great historical document would be absurd, but it does contain more of substance than most false-door texts. It puts Ptahshepses firmly in historical context and suggests that he lived perhaps for seventy to eighty years, an exceptional span for ancient

24

Egypt. There is yet something irresistibly attractive about such a great man who could record of one king, possibly Neferirkare, 'His Majesty allowed me to kiss his foot; his Majesty did not allow me to kiss the ground'. In such points of royal grace could true merit be discerned.

Most Old Kingdom tombs were furnished with one or more statues of the dead owner, the function of which was to act as a surrogate for the deceased if his actual body was destroyed and his spirit in danger of having no base from which to operate posthumously. Not infrequently the tomb-owner is shown with his wife, and even with children – the whole family, as it were, gathered together in death. The statue of Katep and his wife Hetepheres, while not being an outstanding sculpture of the period, is a charming example of the family genre. Katep, a moderately important official with responsibilities over public works, including boundaries, and with a supervisory function over the royal 'ordinary' priests, probably during the Fifth Dynasty, is shown sitting cosily with his wife contemplating eternity. Rather unusually, both are shown at the same height; more commonly the wife is represented less tall than the husband. Hetepheres is shown wearing a fairly plain long gown; her flesh is painted yellow, the conventional colour for ladies in Egyptian art; and she has her left arm around her husband's waist in a gesture of affection. Katep himself wears an elaborate collar and a short kilt; his flesh is, again conventionally, painted red. It is altogether an unglamorous sculpture, but it fulfils admirably its funerary function, representing a very worthy couple, radiating conjugal contentment and satisfaction in lives well spent.

It would be interesting to know what might have been said about Katep and Hetepheres by the subjects of another limestone pair-statue. This later sculpture, more than 1,000 years younger in date, has an unspecified provenance but may be considered to be essentially Memphite and probably from Saqqara on the basis of excavations conducted in recent years by the Egypt Exploration Society in a part of the necropolis devoted to the tombs of very important officials and nobles whose base was Memphis in the Eighteenth and Nineteenth Dynasties. This second couple, also seated side by side, and holding hands, are rather more grand than Katep and Hetepheres. They are shown wearing elaborately pleated clothes and heavy formal wigs, and the chair on which they sit has a high back and finely carved animal legs. The hauteur of the later pair is easily recognised; they are altogether more socially conscious, more cultivated, more refined in their sensibilities, in short, more 'civilised'. They are eighteenth-century city exquisites, in contrast with medieval country freemen. In one matter, however, they would have found themselves seriously disadvantaged compared with Katep and Hetepheres. They have no inscription, and hence no names.

A sculpture without a name carved, or in some other way written, upon it was an ineffective object in ancient Egypt. Katep and Hetepheres have their names cut deep into the base of their statue; in this way it was animated and rendered an efficient instrument for the perpetuation of their posthumous life and identity. It has properly performed its function because its subjects can still be identified as Katep and Hetepheres. The nameless subjects of the later statue-group, on the other hand, will almost certainly remain unidentified unless some extraordinary discovery reveals the sculpture's precise position in the tomb of a named person from which it was removed in the early nineteenth century.

Such an extraordinary discovery seemed to have been made in 1975 when the excavators of the Egypt Exploration Society discovered the tomb of Horemheb, who was perhaps the most important secular official in Egypt during the reign of Tutankhamun. General, Deputy of His Majesty, and Chief Steward, to name the most recognisably important of his titles. Horemheb subsequently became king himself, succeeding the ephemeral Ay in about 1319 BC. While he exercised his high functions of state during Tutankhamun's reign, his base, and his home probably, was the city of Memphis. After a period of relative eclipse during the Middle Kingdom and Second Intermediate Period, Memphis enjoyed a welcome revival of fortunes in the Eighteenth Dynasty. Its status as a political centre was greatly enhanced by the establishment of a second vizierate in the city, with special responsibilities for the administration of Lower Egypt, for the control of trade with Asiatic tributary states, and for the exercise of diplomatic negotiations with the same foreign countries and possibly also with Libya and the islands of the Mediterranean. Memphis became again a powerhouse of political and business activities, as it had been during the great days of the Old Kingdom. Although the physical remains of the city can scarcely be compared with the mighty monuments built at Thebes during the New Kingdom, it is becoming increasingly evident from new discoveries both in the city area and at Saqqara that Memphis was no second-rank provincial centre, but a true second capital of Egypt.

From this important base Horemheb would have considered it right that in due time he should be buried in the Memphite necropolis. He therefore had a wonderful tomb prepared for himself on an imposing high point at Saqqara, from which he would be able after death, when his soul emerged from the tomb by day, to look north over the pyramids and lesser burials of his predecessors as far even as Giza, and south over a similar scene as far as Dahshur. The tomb was laid out in its superstructure very like a small temple, with open courts, colonnades and shrines, and its walls were decorated with reliefs of a quality and interest almost without parallel among non-royal tombs.

27 Egypt Exploration Society excavations in the New-Kingdom cemetery of Saqqara. The tomb of Tia, sister of Ramesses II, is on the right, and that of Horemheb on the left.

28 Crystalline limestone head of an old man, almost life size. Although of Twenty-fifth Dynasty date, it shows archaising features characteristic of Middle-Kingdom sculpture.

Fate, however, stepped in and organised his elevation to the monarchy, translation to Thebes and ultimate burial in the Valley of the Kings, in a tomb of exquisitely carved reliefs but rather dull in its religio-mythical subject matter.

The abandoned Saqqara tomb was certainly used in due course for burials, possibly even of members of Horemheb's family. Subsequently plundered and partially dismantled, particularly to provide stone for the building of the adjacent Coptic monastery of Apa Jeremias, it remained buried and unidentified until the 1820s. Then Saqqara was raked over for transportable antiquities and large parts of Horemheb's tomb found their way into collections and museums throughout the world. In 1835 one fine inscription and two inscribed door jambs, all with finely carved figures of Horemheb, entered the British Museum. At the same time the fine, if supercilious, pair-statue arrived. When the tomb of Horemheb was rediscovered in 1975, a statue podium was found which at first was thought possibly to be the original placement for the unnamed couple. Sadly, the coincidence cannot be established with any certainty, and Mr and Mrs X must endure their anonymity for a further spell of what might have been termed 'negative existence' by the ancient Egyptians.

Since the rediscovery of Horemheb's first tomb, the sepulchres of more very important people of the New Kingdom have been excavated both by the Egypt Exploration Society and by Egyptian archaeologists. High officials and even members of the royal family of Ramesses II were buried at Saqqara, and there can be no doubting the contemporary importance of Memphis. In the reign of the great Ramesses (c. 1290–1224 BC) no man made a greater mark on Memphis than his son Khaemwese, who for a time was designated Crown-Prince. Although he did not live to succeed his father, his activities in the northern capital left him a reputation which endured right down to the Graeco-Roman Period, one thousand years later.

For the whole of his adult life Khaemwese served the great Memphite god Ptah, often thought of as the most practical of Egyptian deities, whose theology was yet more intellectual and less magical (in the crude sense of the word) than those other major theologies connected with the gods Re and Thoth, in particular. During much of his lifetime he held a secondary position under the appointed High Priest of Ptah (a notable example of the Egyptians' respect for authority: it would presumably have been a simple matter for the fourth son of Ramesses II to have ousted Huy, the legitimate pontiff). In due course he did become High Priest and was presumably still in office when he died in about the fifty-fifth year of Ramesses' reign. A wealth of records shows how much he accomplished in his career, and one may be certain that those that survive tell only a small part of the full story. It was traditional for the reigning king to celebrate his jubilees at Memphis. Ramesses departed from tradition and celebrated his renewal festivals at Piramesse in the Delta, but Khaemwese had the honour on five occasions to carry the joyful news throughout the length of Egypt. He was also much concerned with the ceremonies involving the Apis bull, and it was he who supervised the cutting of the first multiple burial-place or catacomb for the dead bulls. Indeed, so attached was he to the Apis cult that it is very probable that his own tomb was incorporated in this catacomb at Saqqara.

It is as a high religious leader that Khaemwese is depicted in a remarkable breccia statue found, not at Memphis, but at Abydos 400 miles to the south. His presence so far from base no doubt indicates his participation in important ceremonies in the temples newly built and completed at Abydos by his father (see Chapter 5). It may be suspected that because of his privileged background Khaemwese was able to operate over a much wider field than any non-royal official, religious or secular. He certainly busied himself with unusual activities like the rehabilitation of ancient monuments in the Memphite necropolis, identifying by inscription for posterity the builders of many of the pyramids.

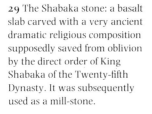

**29** The Shabaka stone: a basalt slab carved with a very ancient dramatic religious composition supposedly saved from oblivion by the direct order of King Shabaka of the Twenty-fifth Dynasty. It was subsequently used as a mill-stone.

30 Diorite statue of Horemheb shown as a scribe. This sculpture, made before Horemheb became king, is thought to have come from Memphis.

At Memphis, in secular role, he appears to have been involved in works connected with shipping. It is highly likely that throughout the New Kingdom, the water-front district of Memphis was the principal Egyptian port, housing docks and shipyards. In the Eighteenth Dynasty it had been called Peru-nefer, and papyrus documents show that huge quantities of timber for ship-building were delivered there.

Perhaps the most remarkable fact about Khaemwese is that his memory and reputation did not fade away after his death. While a continuous record of respect, honour, even worship, cannot be traced from the thirteenth century BC down to the Graeco-Roman Period, it must be assumed that his memory lived on at least in folk tradition for a full thousand years. A series of romances was composed towards the end of the Pharaonic Period, and versions are preserved, written in demotic (one of the scripts found on the Rosetta Stone, a very cursive way of writing Egyptian). In these stories Khaemwese figures as something of a magician and he is familiarly called Setne, a name derived from his actual priestly title in the service of Ptah, *Sem* or *Setem*, later also *Seten*. Papyri in the Cairo Museum recount the adventures of Setne with magicians, including one very bothersome episode in which the great man fancies a lady walking about the precinct of Ptah in Memphis, and gets his servant to proposition her. She, Tabubu by name, turns out to be a priestess of Bastet and she tempts Setne to Bubastis where, apparently, he makes over all his property to her in expectation of pleasures to come; he even kills his children so as not to cause testamentary problems. This nightmare story turns out to be a dream, but Setne is made to look very foolish and is obliged to make reparation to others whom he had tried to trick.

Memphis entered into a new period of first-rank importance after the somewhat chaotic years of the Twenty-first to Twenty-third Dynasties (*c.* 1070–712 BC). Invading puritans from Napata in Nubia, re-establishing unity in Egypt under the Twenty-fifth Dynasty, did much to rehabilitate Memphis. King Piye (or Piankhy) made the initial strike in about 729 BC, in the course of which he captured Memphis with a massive attack from the river side. He made special presentations of booty to the great temple of Ptah, and this respect for one of Egypt's oldest shrines was continued by Shabaka, the first king proper of the Twenty-fifth Dynasty (712–698 BC). One monument which demonstrates this king's concern for the traditions of the past is the so-called Shabaka stone. At first sight this great rectangular slab of basalt looks like nothing more than a nether mill-stone: in the centre is a deep hole from which radiate grooves running to the stone's edge; much of the surface is worn and polished clean. Its condition is indeed due to its having been used to grind grain. Closer insepction, however, reveals in those places where the wear is lightest a shallow carved text set out in the form of a document of the Old Kingdom. According to the introduction it was carved by order of Shabaka to preserve a text of great antiquity written on a worm-eaten original. The composition deals in a somewhat dramatic manner with the Memphite theology of Ptah; it also pronounces the nature and greatness of the god, and the importance of Memphis as the unifier of the whole land of Egypt. Much scholarly debate has revolved around both the nature of the text and its precise date. It has been characterised as a kind of religious drama, one of the most ancient in the world; it has also been interpreted as a straightforward treatise on the religious character of Memphis and its principal god. Traditionally it has been accepted as a late copy of an old document, as is stated on the

29

31 The fine basalt lid of the coffin of Sisobk, Memphite vizier, who was also mayor of Saïs in the Delta early in the Twenty-sixth Dynasty.

32 The grey granite sarcophagus of the high agricultural official Hapmen. It was found in modern times in Cairo where it was used as a water trough and called 'the Lover's Fountain'.

stone itself; recently the suggestion has been made that the whole text is a kind of late fake or confection, deliberately composed in Shabaka's reign to enhance the king's reputation as a respecter of Egypt's ancient religion. The arguments rest on niceties of language in the text, and they have much to commend them. And historically, there is much to be said in favour of the confection theory. There is no doubt that the kings of both the Twenty-fifth and Twenty-sixth Dynasties looked back to earlier periods for inspiration and support, not only in religion but also in political forms, and especially art.

A striking crystalline limestone head which is said to come from Memphis shows 28 splendidly how sculpture of an earlier period was copied, yet subtly modified, during the Twenty-fifth Dynasty. At first sight it might well be taken to be a sensitive portrait of an elderly man, an official towards the end of a long career in which troubles and difficult decisions have wreaked their toll on a handsome face. It is undoubtedly a fine sensitive sculpture, but in its principal features – high cheek-bones, heavy eyelids, large ears and characteristic full wig – it reproduces the hall-marks of certain Middle-Kingdom sculptures, particularly the royal representations of Sesostris III. It is in the best archaising style of the Twenty-fifth Dynasty and must have belonged to a near life-size statue of a man who surely occupied a high position in the bureaucracy of Lower Egypt. This bureaucracy was still headed by the Lower Egyptian vizier, now without a doubt the most important civil officer in the land, but it is very probable that Memphis was not always his seat of power. There was some duality of base.

A powerful early Twenty-sixth-Dynasty vizier, Sisobk, was a priest of Ptah and mayor 31 of Saïs, the principal base of the kings of that dynasty (hence called Saïte). His great and handsome coffin is typical of the massive equipment provided for the burials of the great at this time. In the Memphite necropolis the engineering problems must have been acute. Huge shafts were sunk into the desert plateau and burial chambers with vaulted roofs constructed at their bottoms to accommodate the sarcophagi. It is almost impossible to visualise the exact procedures by which such sepulchres were cut and the great equipments lowered safely to their positions; it is impossible to believe that such operations could have been carried out without substantial human casualties. Even to excavate such tombs is a hazardous business.

33 The camel and horse park below the Great Pyramid at Giza: early morning preparations before the first visitors arrive.

Yet even in earlier times, when the adventurers who broke into tombs had their sights well set on more obvious plunder, coffins from such tombs were removed and taken long distances. When Cairo first became readily accessible to European travellers during the Napoleonic expedition, one such granite coffin was found, in the words of the great *Description de l'Egypte* (the official report in many volumes containing the scientific results of Napoleon's enterprise): 'in the great street leading to the Citadel, close by the mosque of Tulun (Ibn Tulun), a place called Qala't el-Kabsh. It had formerly served as a reservoir or water-trough, as can be seen from the opening cut in one end'. Other accounts regularly describe it as having been called 'the Lover's Fountain' by the Turks. Unhappily the story behind this appellation has not, apparently, been recorded. Could it have been a common place for assignations – the Cairene equivalent of the clock at London's Victoria Station? Its romantic past is worth conjuring up when the reality of the piece is observed: but more prosaically it is the sarcophagus of Hapmen, a Saïte 32 official with many titles indicating his responsibilities for agricultural matters, grain collection and revenue in general. Removed from the mosque of Ibn Tulun by the French, it was included among the antiquities handed over to the British Army at the capitulation of Alexandria in 1801. How it originally arrived in Cairo is beyond discovery, but there is some hope that one day the actual tomb of Hapmen will be discovered. It may be at Saqqara, or even more probably at Giza. One huge multiple sepulchre was excavated by Colonel Howard Vyse not far from the great Sphinx in 1837. Originally it had been prepared for a senior scribal official of the Twenty-sixth Dynasty called Pakap, and later enlarged to take further burials. Among Colonel Vyse's assistants was Giovanni Battista Caviglia, a Genoese sea-captain, who had in 1816–19 made a clearance around the forequarters of the Sphinx from which came fragments of the beard of that creature. Caviglia in the contentious way which often affects archaeological partnerships tried subsequently to take full credit for the discovery. The great burial, which had been thoroughly robbed in ancient times, was at once named Campbell's Tomb, after Colonel Patrick Campbell, British consul-general in Egypt from 1833 to 1840, who was closely associated with Vyse's enterprise and was substantially instrumental in obtaining the necessary permission *(firman)* for the work from Muhammad Ali, Pasha of Egypt. The finest discovery in Campbell's Tomb was the complete sarcophagus of Nesisut, a priestly official in Memphis during the Twenty-seventh Dynasty, a period when Egypt suffered from domination by the Persians (525–404 BC). It is very finely finished and has excellently carved inscriptions and divine representations. The lid, which is highly polished, carries a fine, if somewhat conventional, 'portrait' of the deceased. In all it is a remarkable testimony to the continuity of Egyptian religious practice and technical skill even in times of extreme difficulty.

Some of Colonel Vyse's best and most interesting work was carried out in the Giza pyramids, and possibly his most unusual discovery was that of a wooden coffin cover in the pyramid of Mycerinus – the smallest of the three 'great' Giza monuments, a mini-pyramid by Fourth-Dynasty standards, rising only to about 228 feet in height (the Great Pyramid measuring about 480 feet in height). In the burial chamber of this pyramid, the great stone royal sarcophagus was found, empty, and in an adjacent room, half full of rubbish, interesting 'remains' were unearthed by Mr Raven, Vyse's assistant:

In clearing the rubbish out of the large entrance-room, after the men had been employed there several days, and had advanced some distance towards the south-eastern corner, some bones were first discovered at the bottom of the rubbish; and the remaining bones and parts of the coffin were immediately discovered altogether: no other parts of the coffin or bones could be found in the room; I therefore had the rubbish which had been previously turned out of the same room, carefully re-examined, when several pieces of the coffin and of the mummy-cloth were found; but in no other part of the pyramid were any part of it to be discovered, although every place was mostly minutely examined to make the coffin as complete as possible. There was about three feet of rubbish on the top of the same; and from the circumstances of the bones and parts of the coffin being all found together, it appeared as if the coffin had been brought to that spot, and there unpacked.

The parts of the wooden coffin found by Raven could be assembled to form almost the whole of the lid of a coffin shaped like a mummified person (usually termed anthropoid); a very well-cut inscription contained in a cartouche the name Menkaure, the Egyptian form on which the Greek Mycerinus is based. Not surprisingly Vyse and his Egyptian advisers, particularly Samuel Birch in the British Museum, concluded that the actual inner coffin, which had contained the body of the king, had been found, and that the fragments of a human body were likewise parts of the king's corpse. Coarse woollen cloth

34 Remains of the wooden coffin found in the pyramid of Mycerinus at Giza and inscribed with the king's name. A late replacement probably of Twenty-sixth Dynasty date.

34

was also found in association with the human remains, and was understandably interpreted as mummy wrapping. It was thought, quite correctly, that the coffin had been taken from the great stone sarcophagus, and moved into the adjacent chamber where its contents could be dealt with at leisure.

This general interpretation remained acceptable well into this century, until scholars, who understood both the history of coffin shapes and construction and the development of the hieroglyphic script, pointed out that anthropoid coffins were not used in the Fourth Dynasty, and that the palaeography (that is the individual sign characteristics) of the inscription demanded a much later date, probably about 600 BC, during the Saïte Period. As far as the coffin, at least, was concerned, a perfectly satisfactory explanation could be provided. The interest shown in earlier periods of antiquity during the Twenty-fifth and Twenty-sixth Dynasties has already been alluded to. This interest undoubtedly included the great monuments of the Memphite necropolis. At Saqqara, for example, a new entrance gallery was tunnelled into the centre of the Step Pyramid from its south side, and conservation work apparently carried out to prevent the collapse of internal masonry on to the sarcophagus chamber of King Djoser. In the subterranean corridors of the same monument, some of the fine low reliefs of the king were marked out with grids, presumably so that they could be copied for reproduction elsewhere. It is equally likely that at Giza, the pyramid of Mycerinus was entered at this time, and the burial found to be violated. With proper piety a new inner coffin, suitably, but anachronistically, inscribed was prepared for a reburial just as had happened in Thebes during the Twenty-first Dynasty (see p. 157). Much later, possibly in late antiquity, the pyramid was again entered, but this time by men uninspired by pious benevolence. In the ensuing robbery the coffin was removed from the stone sarcophagus and left broken and abandoned after its contents had been ravaged.

So much for the coffin fragments! What about the parts of a human body with pieces of woollen cloth adhering? It was naturally assumed that here were the pitiful relics of Mycerinus' shattered mummy. Undistinguished in appearance, and embarrassing in their very existence, they lay for over a century in the British Museum, possibly the only Egyptian royal remains outside Egypt itself. Science eventually provided the answer; to some a disappointment, but to most a comforting reassurance. Pieces of bone were measured for age by the Radiocarbon process; the result gave a date of about 1,500 years before the present time, that is during the Roman occupation of Egypt.

A little earlier some cautious comments were made about the mock realism of one sculptural portrait of the Twenty-fifth Dynasty. It reminds us, as indeed almost every ancient Egyptian sculpture reminds us, that living portraiture was not the ideal purpose of human representation in Egyptian art. Although there are 'portraits', generally sculptured, from most periods, which have been identified as such by students of Egyptian art, they are exceptionally rare. What a person wanted in his or her tomb-representation was a 'likeness' to serve as a surrogate in the afterlife. What was fitting, not what was true, was the ideal; the deceased should be recognised through the inscriptions, in particular through the writing of the individual's name; he should be shown, in most cases conventionally, in the prime of life, unblemished and ready to perform the necessary posthumous duties of the surrogate. It is therefore rather idle to attempt to recognise the inhabitants of ancient Memphis in the multitude of statues and relief

35 A Greek inhabitant of the Memphite region. The portrait, painted on a wood panel, shows its subject in the prime of life and wearing her finest jewellery.

'portraits' which exist still in the monuments of Giza and Saqqara and in the museums of the world. Only a few likely true portraits can be mentioned with any confidence: Ankh-haf in Boston, Ka-aper, the 'Sheikh el-beled' and the dwarf Sonb in Cairo, and the squatting scribe in Paris.

Not until the Graeco-Roman Period did a real appreciation of the value of portraiture develop in Egypt, but even those so-called veristic sculptures from Memphis and its necropolis which qualify for consideration do not bring us very close to the teeming crowds which populated the city at the time. As we shall find in the next chapter, true portraits in the form of individual paintings on wooden panels occur from the first to the fourth centuries AD as part of the mummy equipment of members of the cosmopolitan population of the Hellenised cities throughout Egypt. A substantial Greek-speaking community existed in Memphis, and a number of mummies incorporating portraits and of portraits taken from mummies have been found at Saqqara; they probably present us with the closest we may ever get to likenesses of Memphites. A most striking example shows a lady with fine wide eyes 35 and very full lips, wearing a gilded wreath in her hair, pearl earrings and two gold necklaces. Its Saqqara provenance is not confirmed, however, and the same is the case for the whole plainly bandaged mummy of a young man. His portrait depicts him far less dramatically than his fellow lady Memphite. It is rather flatly painted, and he is shown dressed in a simple tunic and with scarcely any distinctive facial features apart from large staring eyes. In his short life he may have observed from the 'superior' culture of his own community (pagan but refined, Greek-speaking but given to burial by mummification) the dying of native Egyptian religion and the first advances of Christianity. The excavations which revealed the Thirtieth-Dynasty temple and sacred animal catacombs in the northern part of Saqqara also uncovered the remains of an early Christian community, including a church. Further south, also on the Saqqara plateau, a very substantial monastery, dedicated to Saint Jeremias, was established, possibly as early as the fourth century. Memphis had always been an important city, and with its necropolis acted as an influential focus in the land. Its slow decline in late antiquity has left scarcely any mark in the main city area. It had done its time, and with the Arab conquest the focus shifted a few miles north and to the east bank of the Nile. In AD 642 Fustat was established as the base of the conquering invaders; in AD 969 Cairo itself was founded.

# CHAPTER THREE
# The Lake and Joseph's River
## THE FAIYUM AND ITS ENVIRONS

EARLY ON in her *Levant Trilogy* Olivia Manning takes a strange, mixed, group of people out of Cairo on a hot summer day, first to visit the pyramids at Giza, and then on to the Faiyum for a picnic. It is a dreary expedition, ending in an unnecessary and contrived tragedy. Very little idea of the Faiyum is given: it is an 'oasis'; it has a good variety of trees, many of them fruit-bearing, which provide shade; it is dusty; there is an open space called a 'Midan', the Arabic word, Persian in origin, used to describe a public square in an Egyptian town. For those who know the Faiyum the picture is unconvincing, and even allowing for the evident dislike which Olivia Manning shows, through her principal character, for Egypt, and for the lack of interest in the landscape as opposed to character, it might be thought that she had never actually gone to this part of Egypt, which lies to the west of the Nile, about fifty miles south of Cairo (by crow or desert road; rather further by way of the Nile Valley).

One may assume, on the basis of no specific evidence, that the scene of the picnic was the main square of Medinet el-Faiyum, the capital of the province and the site of the ancient capital, Shedet in Pharaonic times, Crocodilopolis in Graeco-Roman times, also called Arsinoe after the queen of Ptolemy II Philadelphus. Others have had a rather different view of the place. Colonel Vyse, the discoverer of Campbell's Tomb and the secondary coffin of Mycerinus, made an excursion into the Faiyum in 1837 after an

36 Fishermen by the shores of the Birket Qarun, known in late antiquity as Lake Moeris. The waters of the lake today are heavily saline and support few fresh-water fish.

extended tour of Upper Egypt. His road brought him to Medinet el-Faiyum 'by a bridge built over clear and sparkling streams'. He continues:

The ruins of Antinoe [*sic*], the antient capital, are situated on a high range of hills, at some distance to the north of Medinet, which, in consequence of an abundant supply of water, is surrounded by luxuriant vegetation, and lofty trees. It is also adorned with handsome minarets, contains several good houses, and a well-supplied bazar, and is better built than the generality of Arab towns. On approaching it over the bridge, it brought to my recollection Windsor, and Eton, without possessing any exact resemblance to either of these places.

In spite of the last, incongruous, comment, something of the unusual quality of the Faiyum which still strikes visitors today is conveyed by Vyse's impressions. Water is the dominant element; although it would be a mistake to accept the romantic appellation, 'the Egyptian Lake-District', given to the region by a great German Egyptologist. He was in a sense using one of the ancient descriptions of the Faiyum, To-she, 'Land of the Lake'; but in English 'Lake District' means something more specific and distinctly localised in north-western England, and no comparison can be made between that region of lakes and mountains and the Faiyum.

Water is the element that transforms the Nile Valley into a green thread of rich cultivation running through tawny deserts to east and west of the river. In the valley itself water has mostly a static quality; the river, dammed and barraged, flows slowly and now for much of the year shows little movement; away from the river the canals are still and run straight for mile after mile. In the Faiyum, however, the visitor is immediately struck by moving water, by the sinuous and impressive Bahr Yusuf, 'Joseph's River', which brings Nile water into the region through the Hawara Channel; by running, sparkling streams and pools and even modest waterfalls in the cultivated parts of the depression; by extraordinary water-wheels of a size and kind found nowhere else in Egypt. And most remarkable, although not moving, is the lake itself, the Birket Qarun, glassy and brooding, surrounded by beaches encrusted with salts, the recipient of all the drainage canals in the region, almost as saline as the sea (nearly 150 feet below sea-level), and very smelly. Around this lake in antiquity active communities came and went in a pattern of variation altogether different from the regularity of life in the Nile Valley proper, where the variation was annual and depended on the inundation.

To appreciate the peculiar character of the Faiyum as one of the most interesting and productive provinces of Egypt from the agricultural point of view, the best way to approach is by way of the Hawara Channel; to pass from the Nile Valley, through the rocky barrier which once separated the Faiyum from the main river plain, following the course of the Bahr Yusuf. Very soon the lush cultivation and the rich groves and orchards around the villages proclaim the special quality of the place. But the perspective is limited, the view too concentrated. To appreciate the dramatic nature of the province, approach by the desert road from Giza, and pause on the 'heights' of Kom Aushim to look down on the gleaming lake, stretching westwards to the low-lying hills, and the deep green promise of the cultivated quarter. From Kom Aushim the contrast of the barren and the fertile can best be observed, and the special, bowl-like aspect of the region comprehended.

There is another good reason for pausing at Kom Aushim; it is the site of one of the many towns founded in the Faiyum province during the Ptolemaic Period. Here at

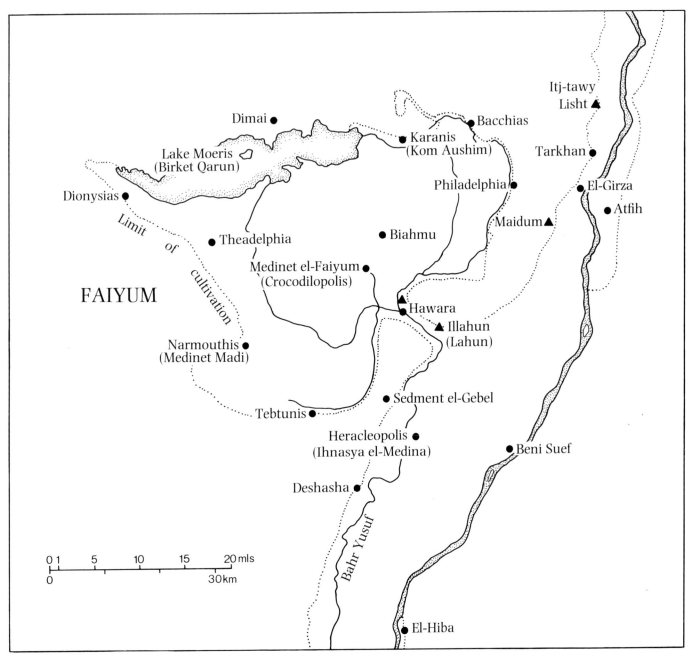

FAIYUM

The Faiyum and its environs.

Karanis it is still possible to walk along streets, to step into houses, to saunter in squares, as one can never do in the Nile Valley itself. For this was a town which fell into disuse and was abandoned in the late Roman Period, to be revealed in modern times by excavations of the University of Michigan. Like its fellow foundations here and elsewhere in Egypt, Karanis was essentially a Greek-speaking town with a mixed population of Greeks and hellenised Egyptians; its methods of administration, of trade and of culture were Greek in general character, but the way of life was very much like that of contemporary Egyptian-speaking towns. On its heights at Kom Aushim, Karanis lies approximately at sea-level, but when it was founded, like many of its fellows, it lay on the edge of the lake, which at that time was about six feet below sea-level. It had been deliberately lowered very

37 A view over the fertile
Faiyum depression from the
desert heights to the north, the
site of the Greek town of
Karanis which flourished from
the first century BC to the fourth
century AD.

considerably in early Ptolemaic times by the construction of barrages in order to reclaim
large tracts of highly productive land. These substantial irrigation works were but the
last in antiquity which were used to manipulate the agricultural capacity of the
province. For two thousand years man had intervened from time to time to change the
shape and depth of the lake, often radically, and usually with remarkable success. Before
about 2000 BC it had been Nature herself who had done the intervening, and also with
radical results from time to time.

The Faiyum depression itself is thought to have been formed by wind erosion,
although there remains some uncertainty on this point. In very remote (Middle
Palaeolithic) times it was filled by water from the Nile by direct connection. Later, as the
bed of the Nile was lowered, the Faiyum became isolated and the lake dried up. Later still
(between Palaeolithic and Neolithic times) the Nile again rose sufficiently to re-establish
the lake at the level of about 60 feet above sea-level – a huge expanse of fresh water
compared with the noisome Birket Qarun of today. During Neolithic times the lake again
receded until it reached a line of about six feet below sea-level; and this remained the level
at which the meagre inflow from the Nile was able to maintain the lake until man began
to take the matter in hand.

Settlements of a relatively advanced Neolithic culture were established along the
north edge of the lake when its surface stood at about 32 feet above sea-level. Their

inhabitants practised agriculture, planting barley and emmer-wheat of quite advanced types, and storing their surpluses in underground silos lined with woven basket-work. One very interesting implement recovered from the scanty remains of these primitive farmers is a sickle; it is quite unlike the sickles of historic Egypt which were curved and angled craftily to make the action of cutting easy. Like historic sickles, however, it is set with shaped flints which provide the cutting edges. The early Faiyum sickle is a straight rod of tamarisk wood, with a short cut along about one-third of its length in which three flints are set. The flints are serrated, rather carelesly, but firmly fixed in position by some resinous substance, and the cutting edges show the polishing characteristically found on flints used for cutting the stalks of cereal crops. A date of about 4000–5000 BC has traditionally been assigned to the culture, commonly called Faiyum A, but a radiocarbon date obtained from a specimen of wood recovered from the same site as the sickle has lowered the acceptable dating to the mid-fourth millennium BC.

Although the settlement of the Faiyum during the first thousand years of the Dynastic Period can be confirmed from archaeological discoveries, mostly around the verges of the depression, little has been found to suggest that any serious exploitation of the region was attempted. As so often with the history of ancient Egypt, arguments proceed from silence by way of tantalising textual hints back to silence. The tendency to over-interpret modest evidence ever threatens the unwary historian; for Egypt the tendency amounts at times to overwhelming pressure. The progressive stages of the historical narrative of a country or region need to be set out in tidy order. For the Faiyum the gaps are so huge that to leap them with historical invention is not just hazardous, but outright foolish. There is evidence that Shedet, the forerunner of Crocodilopolis, was a very early foundation and that the cult of the crocodile-god Sobk (for the Greeks, Sukhos) was perhaps of even greater antiquity. But there is no evidence of substantial constructions or

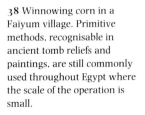

**38** Winnowing corn in a Faiyum village. Primitive methods, recognisable in ancient tomb reliefs and paintings, are still commonly used throughout Egypt where the scale of the operation is small.

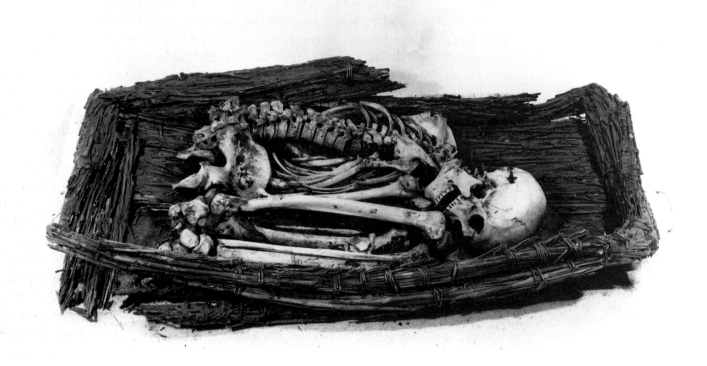

**39** Skeleton in a reed tray – a primitive coffin – from the Early-Dynastic cemetery at Tarkhan.

of important historical events – using the term 'historical' in the unfashionable sense of 'political'. It may indeed be the case that life in the Faiyum during the third millenium BC was uneventful, undeveloped and unexciting; that the modest inflow of water from the Nile allowed little more than subsistence agriculture; that it was a backwater saved from total neglect only by the existence of the cult of Sobk.

Plenty, however, was happening just outside the Faiyum where several important provincial cities had developed in the early Old Kingdom. The district on the west bank of the Nile extending over twenty miles and starting at a point about forty miles south of Memphis seems to have had substantial concentrations of population in late predynastic times and during the early dynasties. At El-Girza in the barren slopes of the desert ridge on the same latitude as the southern shore of the Faiyum lake, Petrie excavated a cemetery with burials of very distinctive and coherent types. From the place he took the name Gerzean, which he assigned to what he regarded as the northern and later phase of predynastic cultures. At Tarkhan, a few miles to the north in the same gravelly slopes, he found an extensive cemetery of the first two dynasties with modest graves, very different in scale and contents from the great contemporary tombs he had found at Abydos and Naqada and those excavated by Emery at Saqqara. Here at Tarkhan, burials were made in relatively shallow graves, with sides revetted with wickerwork, the bodies often laid in shallow rush-woven open coffins in the crouched position typical of predynastic times, but soon to be generally abandoned for all but the simplest burials in dynastic times.

The importance of this district at this early period is obscure; but it seems to have been populous and to have had associations, quite unfathomable at present, with the metropolis of Memphis to the north. South of El-Girza, at Maidum, a remarkable pyramid was built, possibly for Snofru, first king of the Fourth Dynasty, (c. 2575–2551 BC), or for Huni, the last king of the preceding dynasty (c. 2599–2575 BC). Standing high on the desert plateau, this pyramid presents a strange image seen from the valley-road or, through palm-groves, from the train ploughing to Upper Egypt. Isolated, truncated, with much of its outer layers collapsed into piles of rubble, it looks more like the keep of a medieval castle than a proper pyramid. It is not, however, as isolated as it seems. There is at least one huge mud-brick *mastaba* of Third-Dynasty date, others of the same period or earlier, and a number of important, partly stone-built, *mastabas* of members of Snofru's family. Some very good reason, no doubt, led to the choice of Maidum for such important burials, but it was certainly not proximity to Memphis. Two tombs in particular have yielded works of outstanding importance for the history of Egyptian art in the early Old Kingdom. In the tomb of Rahotpe, a son of Snofru, was found by Mariette an extraordinary pair of painted statues of the tomb-owner and his wife, Nofret. Perfect in preservation, pristine and glowing in colour, they provide one of the visitor's most vivid impressions among the wonders of the Old Kingdom in the Cairo Museum. A limestone panel from the same tomb, and now in the British Museum, carries a scene which includes texts carved with hieroglyphic signs of exquisite quality. It shows the prince Rahotpe seated on a low stool with bull-shaped legs, a table loaded with bread offerings set in front of him. An elaborate tabulation of offerings of various kinds occupies the right-hand quarter of the central scene, and various other offerings are named in the field above and below the table; inscriptions in large hieroglyphs in single lines above and at both sides of the scene list Rahotpe's titles and dignities. Paint originally provided detail and contrast to the scene and inscriptions and gave sense to certain elements which are now rather meaningless without colour; thus the garment worn by Rahotpe would originally have been seen as made of leopard-skin, or to simulate the same. The loss of paint has, however, revealed the purity of the carved representations and hieroglyphic signs and the subtlety of the carving of bodily contours and musculature; even the small human figures in the inscriptions show sensitive modelling; the birds are plump and very convincing; the animal-heads display full and fleshy jowls.

Close by Rahotpe and Nofret in the Cairo Museum is the painting which has been considered among the greatest accomplishments of Egyptian graphic art. Nina de Garis Davies, the outstanding copyist of Egyptian painting, had no doubt about its qualities: 'Such is the mastery of its execution, such the craftsman's command of his materials, that it might well stand at the apex of the long centuries of achievement rather than at their base'. It is the 'Maidum Geese', also found by Mariette, but in the tomb of another son of Snofru, Nefermaat, and his wife Itet. Something of the quality of the work of the master who painted in this tomb can be seen in two fragments found subsequently by Flinders Petrie and presented by him to the Victoria and Albert Museum, but now transferred to the British Museum. One shows part of a bird-trapping scene with a masterly painting of a decoy-duck; the other has part of a representation of an attendant leading forward an adax-antelope. In both of these tantalisingly incomplete fragments the painter's unusual exploitation of a relatively limited range of pigments is strikingly demonstrated; in fact he makes the Egyptian palette appear to be infinite in possibility.

Maidum lay in territory belonging to the Twentieth nome of Upper Egypt, the capital city of which was Neni-nesu or Ninsu, called Heracleopolis by the Greeks and Ihnasya el-

40 Painting of geese grazing, from the tomb of Nefermaat and Itet at Maidum. Technically and artistically this is one of the earliest and finest of surviving Egyptian paintings.

Medina today. Historically its moment of greatest glory came during the First Intermediate Period, that time of political disintegration which followed the collapse of strong central government at the end of the Sixth Dynasty (*c.* 2150 BC). For almost one hundred years the rulers of Heracleopolis assumed royal powers and controlled most of Lower Egypt and Upper Egypt almost as far south as Thebes. They are assigned to the Ninth and Tenth Dynasties and many were called Akhtoy (or Khety). Before their time of greatness the rulers or nomarchs of Heracleopolis administered their territory very much under the eye of the central government at Memphis, fifty miles to the north. The place was, however, sufficiently far from the metropolis to have its own necropolis where important local officials might be buried. It lies at Sedment el-Gebel, a few miles to the west of the town on an exposed ridge separating the Nile Valley from the Faiyum to the south of the Hawara Channel.

From one of the tombs of the Sixth Dynasty comes the finest example of Old Kingdom sculpture in the British Museum, the ebony statue of Meryrehashtef. It is one of three statues from the tomb in which the deceased is shown at various stages in his life – youth, middle age (in Copenhagen), and old age (in Cairo). This in itself is unusual because it was generally the case that a tomb-statue represented the deceased in the prime of life, in the condition in which he would hope to pass his afterlife. There are many unusual features about the London statue, which represents the young Meryrehashtef. In the first place it is carved from a single piece of wood (apart from the base), whereas most wooden statues were made in parts, the arms usually being jointed on to the torso at the shoulders. This latter procedure made the sculptor's task much easier, and any imperfections at the joints could be covered up with gesso-plaster and painted. Most wooden sculptures were plastered and painted as the common practice, but in the present case the use of ebony was itself uncommon, and such fine material needed no concealment. Again, it was not common to depict a man in the nude: it might be thought that such a presentation would be acceptable for the youthful Meryrehashtef, but in fact all three statues show him without dress of any kind.

In Egyptian sculpture in general the head was thought to be the most important part of a statue because it contained most visibly the identity of the subject. Heads therefore constitute the most studied elements of Egyptian statues and are usually the parts which command initial attention. The head of the young Meryrehashtef is indeed striking, with its wry smile and fine bold features; but it is not noticeably more so than a great many other heads of the same period. What is much more striking is the body; the sculptor has

**42** *(below)* The great mud-brick *mastaba*-superstructure of a tomb in the early Old-Kingdom cemetery by the pyramid of Snofru at Maidum. The identity of the tomb-owner has never been established.

**41** Fragment of a bird-catching scene from the tomb of Nefermaat and Itet. The first man holds a decoy duck, while the second holds a rope controlling a clap net.

**43** *(below)* Meryrehashtef as a young man. A sculpture in ebony, carved from a single piece of wood (apart from the base), it displays a fine understanding of human anatomy.

**44** *(opposite)* The head of the limestone statue of the overseer of missions, Nenkheftka, whose tomb was at Deshasha; an excellent example of conventional portraiture of the Old Kingdom.

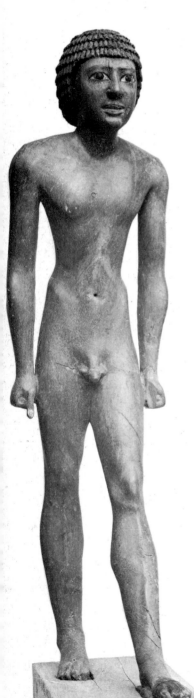

here produced no run-of-the-mill carving, with torso solidly presented, arms pressed closely to the sides, legs firmly set on the ground with the left placed forward at the conventional short stride. Instead he has carved a figure which totally belies the common expectation of the male body in Egyptian art. It is not solid; the arms are free, slightly flexed and move as with a moving body; the legs can be seen to be taking the weight of the man in motion, the left leg being somewhat elongated to promote this impression. The modelling of flesh and muscle is extraordinary, and can be appreciated even more from the back, where the leg muscles, taut buttocks and shoulder-blades all suggest the lithe energy of a young man in active motion. There is even a twist in the torso, which is quite unusual in Egyptian sculpture and which is apparently a required effect and not the result of the warping of the wood. The best comment on the piece is that provided by Henry Moore, who on more than one occasion asked specially to examine it out of its case: 'What I admire about this statue is its tension. If you run your hands down the legs or across the shoulder blades you can feel the tautness and hardness of the muscles. The Egyptian sculptor has squeezed tense physical energy into the whole piece.'

About ten miles to the south of Sedment el-Gebel is another Old-Kingdom necropolis associated with the nome of Heracleopolis. Here at Deshasha, the desert hills lie about two miles back from the cultivation in the Nile Valley and a sandy, barren expanse rises gradually to the quite abrupt scarp where tombs of the Fifth and Sixth Dynasties were prepared, some cut into the cliff face, others with *mastaba* superstructures. One tomb was made for Inti, a royal official engaged in foreign business. An episode from his career involving the capture of an Asiatic town – a most unusual subject for the period – is depicted with much interesting military detail: the fortified town, practically deserted by its male population who are being comprehensively beaten outside in the open field, is assaulted by mine and siege-ladder; within, the ladies left behind set upon those who manage to enter the town in a most spirited manner; some intruders are stabbed, others are obliged to surrender, breaking their bows as an act of submission. Unfortunately the substantial text accompanying the scene is mostly destroyed and, as so often, we are left with but part of the story and a fatal urge to fill in the gaps.

One of Inti's colleagues who was also buried at Deshasha was Nenkheftka; they were both overseers of missions. To contemplate the almost life-size statue of Nenkheftka is to approach some understanding of the power and intelligence of such officials. He is alert, ready to serve the slightest suggestion of action, eager to be away on one of his missions. Carved in limestone and still preserving much of its paint, the statue lacks the fluidity and grace of Meryrehashtef's youthful ebony figure, but it shows great potential to power; it is excellently carved in a pose which itself represented the personification of male activity, and demonstrates again that tension which Henry Moore found so characteristic of the best Egyptian sculpture.

If we return to Heracleopolis, to the town as it was at its time of glory, we visit a place which might have seemed strangely un-Egyptian. This assessment is necessarily one which will be difficult to justify with complete conviction. In general the ancient Egyptians appear to have been an optimistic race. Greatly favoured by the environmental conditions of their country, confident in the special quality of life in the Nile Valley, provided with gods who were individual for Egypt, ruled mostly by autocratic kings with

44

45 A modern mud-brick dovecote in the Faiyum, looking like an elaborate Victorian dessert. Pigeons were reared in antiquity, as today, for the production of fertiliser, not flesh.

a benevolent ethic of power, they enjoyed a remarkably safe and comfortable existence during their lifetimes and could look forward to a continuation of the same after death. The picture is one of near complacence and is applicable principally to those levels of society best able to take advantage of what was offered. At the end of the Old Kingdom this ideal régime collapsed. The reasons for the dramatic dissolution of central control remain undetermined; but there is abundant evidence to show that for at least one hundred years a kind of chaos visited the land accompanied by the kinds of disaster which followed the relaxation of central authority. There may have been incursions of foreigners; there was certainly a collapse of the well-regulated system of irrigation, the effects of which were intensified by a series of low inundations and sporadic famine. Egypt ceased to be not just a great nation, but even a land with an identity; things were not as they had been, and the certainties of life largely evaporated. In fact, life in Egypt at its highest expectation ceased to be Egyptian in the traditional sense. And out of this sad, uncertain, condition came some of the best and most thoughtful literature ever produced in ancient Egypt; literature which was essentially doom-laden and of a flavour not unreminiscent of much that was composed by the Old Testament prophets.

The new centre of power at Heracleopolis, diminished in its influence compared with the Memphis of the Old Kingdom, became a kind of cultural capital. Compositions which later became the earliest 'classics' of Egyptian literature, like *The Instruction of Merikare* (an Heracleopolitan king of the Tenth Dynasty) and the *Dialogue of a man with his soul* were almost certainly composed with the time of disaster in mind, and even in the milieu of the temporary metropolis of Heracleopolis. Many other literary compositions of the subsequent Middle Kingdom derived some of their tone from such depressing tracts, although the later works show strong tendencies to optimism: brighter expectations keep breaking through. It is nevertheless clear that the gloom of the First Intermediate Period left lasting effects and the unusual promotion of Heracleopolis gave the city an importance which also made its mark in literature.

Heracleopolis was the scene of one of the most popular Middle Kingdom stories (said to be such because as many as four papyrus copies of it have survived from antiquity, three of which are in Berlin, and one, sadly fragmentary, in the British Museum: so may popularity be judged). It tells of a farmer called Khunanpu who sets out from his home in the Wadi Natrun, a region of dried-up salt lakes to the north of the Faiyum, to sell his produce in the Nile Valley. He is making for Ninsu, Heracleopolis, but runs into trouble at an unidentified place called Perfefi north of Medenyt. Most commentators have assumed that the wretched man travelled straight to the Nile Valley, presumably striking it north of Memphis, and then following the river south to Ninsu. But what peasant would wish to take such a route, passing several important towns, not least of which was Memphis, in order to dispose of his goods? It seems more likely that he travelled south from the Wadi Natrun to the Faiyum intending to cross this relatively unpopulated region to arrive in the Nile Valley close to Ninsu. One is tempted to see the modern Medinet el-Faiyum in the ancient Medenyt, but the identification should be resisted without further evidence; names can be very seductive. The route, however, is for us of little importance. Ninsu, Heracleopolis, is the goal.

As Khunanpu went along he came to the land owned by a man whose name has traditionally been given as Djehutinakhte, but may, perhaps more correctly, be Nemtinakhte. This landowner took a fancy to the peasant's donkeys and led him into a trap so that he might have to forfeit them. A cloth was laid across the public path, one end lying in water, presumably a canal or stream, the other touching the barley on the landowner's property. Khunanpu was obliged to drive his donkeys around the cloth on the barley side and one of the donkeys took a mouthful of the crop as he went past. The landowner had him trapped; in spite of all protestations Khunanpu was forced to hand over his donkeys and spent ten days protesting and offering to pay reasonable compensation. He then went on alone to Ninsu to put his case to the chief steward, Rensi, who was so pleased by the eloquence of the peasant that he kept him for days listening to his pleas and petitions; in the meanwhile making sure that Khunanpu's wife in the Wadi Natrun was being properly looked after. After the ninth set of petitions the peasant was summoned into the presence of Rensi. Full of apprehension he was made to listen to a

46 One of the columns from the Temple of Arsaphes at Heracleopolis, now standing in front of the museum in Adelaide, South Australia. It carries scenes of Ramesses II offering to ram-headed Arsaphes; also texts added by Merenptah.

transcript of his nine petitions, and then to wait while a set was sent to King Nebkaure, one of the Akhtoy kings of the Tenth Dynasty. He in turn was delighted by the peasant's loquacity and gave Rensi authority to deal with the case. The matter was in due course settled in the peasant's favour and the landowner was himself dispossessed of all his property, which was handed over to Khunanpu. So was justice done.

Although Ninsu's period of supreme importance lasted a relatively short time, it certainly left its mark on Egyptian literature, and on other practices which surprisingly survived the ultimate downfall of the local dynasty at the hands of the Theban rulers of the late Eleventh and Twelfth Dynasties. During the period of Heracleopolitan ascendancy the local deity Herishef (in Greek Arsaphes) achieved an importance well outside the immediate geographical area of his domain. It was no uncommon thing, even in Thebes during the early Middle Kingdom, to include in private letters greetings which invoked this god: 'May Arsaphes, Lord of Heracleopolis, help you', and 'May your repute be good with the spirit (*ka*) of Arsaphes, Lord of Heracleopolis'. There seems little doubt that the impact made in Egypt by this important city and its local deity, was much greater than the surviving evidence would suggest. There is even a sneaking feeling that a deliberate attempt may have been made during the Middle Kingdom to wipe from the record any good achievements notched up in the Twentieth nome. Much, however, remains to be done archaeologically on the site, seriously despoiled although it has been by local farmers and merchants who have pillaged the ancient remains for fertilising soil and building material. Flinders Petrie, who worked for one season there in 1904, had a very sorry tale to tell of his difficulties with the representatives of local farmers;

We had continual trouble with the contractor who annually purchases from the Antiquity Department the right to destroy the Roman buildings for bricks. The whole of the walls of the Roman age are mined out by long underground burrows; and the large piles of red bricks thrown up for sale to distant places show the sites of churches and mansions of which no one will ever know more. This contractor claimed to destroy immediately all the walls we uncovered and incessant feuds, alarms, and nightly plunderings went on. At last I confiscated all the tools of any men caught in our workings. After getting half a dozen picks and baskets, and facing out a long discussion with a prevaricating assembly of parties interested, my work was left in comparative peace.

Petrie writes lightly of his troubles but there is no concealing his disgust at what was going on. There is even less left today, and one can hardly grumble at the removal from the temple site of a number of fallen granite columns excavated by Edouard Naville in 1891. These columns were taken with the permission of the Antiquities Service and now can be seen in museums from Manchester to Adelaide, from Boston to London. The example in the British Museum is splendidly preserved, a monolithic shaft with palm-leaf capital. Its principal inscriptions and scenes are of the reign of Ramesses II and include fine representations of the king with Arsaphes, shown in human form with ram-head. Secondary texts have been added by Merenptah (*c.* 1224–1214 BC), Ramesses' son and successor. This and the other transported columns may, however, have formed part of a Middle Kingdom temple on the same site. Re-use of building material in Egypt was no new discovery of the late nineteenth century.

Although the kings of the Twelfth Dynasty were from the south, perhaps even natives of Thebes, they very prudently paid a great deal of attention to the northern parts of

47 Large numbers of terracotta figurines were manufactured in the towns of the Faiyum in Graeco-Roman times. Here, on the left, is a double oil lamp supported by a figure of the god Bes, and on the right, a slave among vines, turning an Archimedes screw (a device for raising water) with his feet.

Egypt and particularly to the region around Heracleopolis and the neighbouring Faiyum. A new capital, Itj-tawy, 'Seizer of the Two Lands', was founded at Lisht, about forty miles to the north of Heracleopolis, and a new royal Residence was established. One very important result of this change of focus was the development of the Faiyum during the Twelfth Dynasty. There is much uncertainty about what actually happened, and caution has to be exercised in deciding what the contribution of the Twelfth Dynasty kings actually was. The generally accepted story is that one king, possibly Ammenemes III (c. 1844–1797 BC), or even Ammenemes I (c. 1991–1962 BC) took steps to revive agriculture in the Faiyum by increasing and regulating the inflow of water.

The principal written source for this project of irrigation is, surprisingly, the Greek historian Herodotus, and the unpredjudiced reader may well wonder why so much credence is given to his account in this respect when so often his historical narrative concerning Egypt is, to say the least, shaky in authority. As ever, he relates something he has heard, and, as often, there was surely some measure of truth in what he had been told. He describes the Faiyum depression as if it were man-made and gives some details about the extent and depth of the lake, also mentioning two huge pyramids which rise out of the water, each supporting a colossal statue. Of the lake itself he says: 'Now the water in the lake does not come from a natural spring (for the land there is extraordinarily parched), but runs in from the Nile through a canal; and for six months it flows inwards into the lake, and for six months outwards to the Nile again.' What is to be made of this description, and how can it be squared with the independent testimony of ancient Egyptian monuments and of geology? If Herodotus had visited the Faiyum himself in the fifth century BC he would indeed have seen a lake much greater than that of

48 The red-painted cartonnage coffin 'shell', embellished with gilded Egyptian funerary motifs, made for the Graeco-Egyptian Artemidorus. The valedictory inscription reads 'O Artemidorus farewell!'.

today, and certainly than that of the period before the Middle Kingdom. Archaeological evidence confirms that the kings of the Twelfth Dynasty were active in the Faiyum depression, and the limestone traces of two huge colossi of Ammenemes III can still be seen at Biahmu a few miles from Shedet, the district capital. Petrie found fragments of the statues themselves – sandstone seated figures – and he formed the opinion after careful examination that the limestone bases originally took the form of truncated pyramids, 21 feet high, while the statues themselves were at least 35 feet high over and above the bases. These impressive monuments must certainly be the pyramids described by Herodotus, and it is now thought that the statues were raised to this height so that they would appear well above high-water level when the lake was at its fullest, during the time of the Nile inundation.

Some reasonable reconstruction of events may then be made which would to a great extent justify Herodotus' account. The canal he describes running into the Faiyum is the Bahr Yusuf which still today feeds water into the depression through the Hawara Channel. It must be assumed that during the Twelfth Dynasty the flow of the Bahr Yusuf was improved to such an extent that water from the Nile passed into the Faiyum so plentifully during the time of inundation every year that eventually an equilibrium was established between the level of the lake and that of the Nile itself. From then onwards, the inflow during the inundation not only made up any losses by evaporation during the rest of the year but also allowed excessive amounts of water in years of high Nile to be diverted into the natural Faiyum basin. Then after the inundation, surplus waters from the Faiyum could flow back into the Nile Valley to supplement the lower level of the main stream. In this way the Faiyum became a very fertile and productive province ideally sited to provide produce for the greatly increased local population in the neighbourhood of the new capital of Itj-tawy. Almost equally important were the improved fisheries in the lake.

The one puzzling element in this account is the Bahr Yusuf, 'Joseph's River'. Throughout history, in fact, its nature and function give rise to many questions. Its name is wholly without explanation. Yusuf (Joseph) could be the Biblical Joseph, the name having been applied apocryphally because of the steps he had taken to preserve Egypt from famine; this could be folk-memory at work. It has also been suggested that the original Yusuf was the hydraulic engineer who masterminded the Twelfth Dynasty works – something rather desperate here. The true explanation – if there is one – is probably beyond recovery now. But what is this Bahr Yusuf? Although today it has been modified and controlled, it is still essentially a branch of the Nile, flowing from the main stream at Deirut in Middle Egypt, about 150 miles to the south of the Faiyum, and winding north in a very sinuous course, following a general line several miles to the west of the Nile. It has been suggested that it was originally man-made, but the sinuosity of its course almost conclusively disproves this idea. No man-made canal in Egypt is, or was, other than straight in its general course. It is, as geologists would now probably agree, natural in origin, a kind of overflow course which had developed into a feeder of the Faiyum in the days after the waters of the Nile were ultimately confined to the main valley. Its function of feeding the Faiyum lake could only be properly exercised when the entrance to the Faiyum depression through the Hawara Channel – the natural break through the ridge separating the Nile Valley from the Faiyum – was deep enough to

49 The Hawara pyramid of King Ammenemes III overlooking the place where the Bahr Yusuf flows into the Faiyum. In front of the pyramid was a great and splendid temple, known in late antiquity as the Labyrinth.

allow an ample inflow. The silting up of the Bahr Yusuf at this point had resulted, as we observed earlier, in the lowering of the lake to about six feet below sea-level. At this level it remained until the Middle Kingdom.

It is generally believed now that the works which transformed the Faiyum into a fertile province with a greatly increased lake consisted not in the construction of dykes and barrages, but simply in the deepening of the Hawara Channel. So would the Nile re-enter the Faiyum plentifully during the inundation, gradually filling up the lake until an equilibrium between lake and flooded Nile Valley was once again achieved. There were many high Niles during the initial period of refilling and it may not have taken many years to reach equilibrium. The surface of the lake then fluctuated between 60 and 70 feet above sea-level, and so it remained down to the Ptolemaic Period. With such depths of water it is estimated that the pyramidal bases of the colossi of Biahmu would have been about half submerged during the height of the flood.

Whichever of the Twelfth Dynasty kings effected this transformation, it is certain that Ammenemes III had a particular attachment to the region. Apart from the Biahmu colossi, he built a huge pyramid for his tomb at Hawara, not far from the Bahr Yusuf, and a funerary temple adjacent to the pyramid which was so vast and impressive that it was known in late antiquity as the Labyrinth. Its position is now marked by a huge wasted area, dug over, pitted and piled up, looking more like an abandoned industrial dump than the site of a structure of surpassing beauty and interest. Can this be the building of which Herodotus said: 'I visited it and saw it to be beyond words. For if the walls and the remarkable works of the Greeks were put all together they would not seem to be the equal of this Labyrinth in labour and expense.'?

The lake remained at the high level of the Middle Kingdom for well over 1,500 years, and was then, as it seems, deliberately lowered to about six feet below sea-level in the early Ptolemaic Period (first half of the third century BC), as reported earlier in this chapter. It was probably no longer thought necessary, or even desirable, that the Faiyum should continue to act as an escape 'sump' for excess flood-waters. As part of the development of Egyptian agriculture by the Ptolemies, extra water was needed for the lands bordering the Delta; while the land reclaimed by lowering the Faiyum lake was specially fertile and available to support the new towns founded around the lake of Moeris, as it was now called. This name Moeris is the Greek form of the ancient Egyptian Mi-wer, 'Great Channel', which anciently designated a town at the point where the Bahr Yusuf turned westwards through the Hawara Channel. It is a case of the strange way in which a place-name can be taken from the waterway on which it stands, just as Kingston-upon-Hull is commonly called Hull – a telling comparison made by Sir Alan Gardiner, who satisfactorily established the location of Mi-wer.

Life in the Faiyum in the Graeco-Roman Period was centred administratively on the Ptolemaic foundations, the inhabitants of which were of mixed race but culturally hellenised. Nothing indicates the tenacity of the Egyptian element in this racial mixture more than the funerary practices revealed by the burials in the cemeteries associated with the new towns. The common procedure was to carry out a form of mummification of the dead person – a miserable travesty of the best techniques of the Pharaonic Period – which ended up with a carefully bandaged body over the face of which was placed a painting of the deceased, done in many cases from life. In the last chapter the mummy-portraits found at Saqqara were seen to offer the most life-like representations of Memphites. The portrait gallery of Faiyumic inhabitants of the early centuries AD is far and away more striking and varied. More burials with portraits have been found in the Faiyum than anywhere else in Egypt; so much so that such paintings, even those which may have come from elsewhere are commonly called Faiyum portraits.

The biggest find was made in the 1880s, apparently in the cemeteries of the northern Faiyum towns, especially Philadelphia. They were excavated illicitly on behalf of a Viennese collector, Theodor Graf, and, archaeologically speaking, are almost worthless as a group, even though many are artistically outstanding. The best information about the nature of the burials in which the portraits were used came from the excavations carried out by Flinders Petrie at Hawara in two seasons in 1888 and 1911. The huge Roman cemetery lies to the north of the pyramid of Ammenemes III and the 'Labyrinth', and it contained the burials of people from Crocodilopolis, or Arsinoe as it was called from Ptolemaic times. Petrie thought, with good reason, that the prepared mummies with their portraits were kept unburied for some time before being interred, perhaps in groups. The portraits, prepared in advance of death, were cut down from larger panels when they were fitted in the bandaging. In their use one may recognise the ancient Egyptian wish to maintain personal identity after death. In fact this relatively superficial purpose seems to have been paramount, for the preparation of the body was perfunctory. All the skill went into presentation. One very well-prepared mummy of a youth with a good, sensitive, portrait contains a miserably confused set of bones. The body must have been reduced almost to a skeleton before the mummy was made. But through the portrait, which like most was painted in a technique using beeswax as the medium (generally, but rather misleadingly called the 'encaustic' process), the youth lives on, wide-eyed and fresh-faced.

48    Of all the Hawara burials found by Petrie, the most spectacular and culturally revealing is that of a man called Artemidorus. X-ray examination has shown that he was young at the time of death, possibly in his early twenties; the condition of the body is disordered, but not in quite such disarray as that of the wide-eyed youth. Yet he was buried in very considerable style. His bandaged body has been encased within a plaster 'shell' stained a rich reddish pink, on which are modelled in gilded plaster relief scenes taken straight from the native ancient Egyptian funerary repertory: the god of embalming, Anubis, completes the mummification of the deceased, supported by two goddesses, Isis and Nephthys; the gods Horus and Thoth support the fetish of Osiris, the divine king of the after-life; the god Osiris, mummified but sitting up in anticipation, is visited sexually by Isis in the form of a bird. Above the top scene a short text in Greek reads 'O Artemidorus, farewell!' The splendid plaster shell also provides the dead young man with an elaborate gilded collar terminating in divine falcon heads. Most striking, however, is the 'encaustic' wax portrait of Artemidorus. Again a sensitive rendering, conveying the impression of a thoughtful subject, it is executed with very considerable painterly skill, lacking the naïve charm of many of the less accomplished examples of the genre. There are more highlights, and by the use of shading and a more varied palette the portrait has greater depth than most. Artemidorus was certainly from a family of some status – a probability made more likely by the circumstances of his burial – and status is made apparent in the richness of the mummy and especially by the gold wreath he wears on his head. His short life was completed in the early second century AD, when the hold of ancient Egypt's funerary traditions still clearly meant something, even in cosmopolitan Arsinoe.

Changing fortunes have affected the Faiyum since the earliest times, and for the last five thousand years the changes can be traced with a fair degree of accuracy. Too much water has meant good, but limited cultivation; too little water has led to barrenness; best conditions have followed careful control over the Bahr Yusuf at its entrance into the depression. In antiquity it was probably best administered hydraulically in the Ptolemaic and Roman Periods. In modern times, after centuries of neglect following the Islamic

51 A fine portrait of a woman, painted on canvas and not cut down to fit over the face of a mummy; a tempera, not wax 'encaustic' work.

conquest of Egypt, the aim is to maintain the lake, the Birket Qarun, at low level to ensure the efficient drainage of the cultivated area. This result is achieved by the strict limitation of the inflow of water by locks and barrages – a task made easier by the elimination of the annual inundation after the building of the High Dam south of Aswan. And so the lake has become a vast sump, very saline, and, as we said earlier, very unpleasant. Its fresh-water fishing is about finished; its sea-water fishing is just developing. Nature has here provided a compensating answer to a special problem; but will this particular answer survive for many years the inescapable build-up of chemical fertilisers in that baneful mere?

# CHAPTER FOUR

# Provincial Dignitaries

## MIDDLE EGYPT

THERE IS Upper Egypt and there is Lower Egypt. Upper Egypt is the lower part of Egypt on the map, Lower Egypt is at the top. The division is very ancient, preceding, in idea if not in administrative fact, the unification of the whole of Egypt by Menes at the beginning of the First Dynasty. During historic times Upper Egypt started at Elephantine at the First Cataract on the Nile (present-day Aswan) and ended just south of Memphis, while Lower Egypt began at Memphis and included everything to the north. But eventually Lower Egypt came to be the Delta and Upper Egypt the main Nile Valley. So it is today: everything south of Cairo is now Upper Egypt, and even a letter addressed to an archaeologist working at Saqqara may be addressed to Upper Egypt. On the other hand, Lower Egypt is no longer much used for the northern part of the country and it would not normally be put on an envelope addressed to someone in Mansura in the middle of the Delta.

What then is Middle Egypt? It is perhaps easier to say what it is not, than to determine precise limits. There was no Middle Egypt in ancient times. There is no Middle Egypt as an administrative region in modern times. It may be supposed that to most modern Egyptians the idea of a Middle Egypt would be meaningless. The term is truly used almost exclusively in archaeological circles and may even derive directly from the division of the country into inspectorates of the Antiquities Service. For the Egyptologist, Middle Egypt is the long stretch of the Nile from Memphis down to just short of Abydos, about 350 miles south of Cairo; it is the part of the country which, until fairly recently, was not much visited by the tourist. South of Memphis and its necropolis, the next principal site was taken to be Abydos. When Arthur Weigall, an Inspector-General of Antiquities for Upper Egypt, produced his *Guide to the Antiquities of Upper Egypt* in 1910, his limits were 'from Abydos to the Sudan frontier'. For him Middle Egypt stopped at Baliana (the river-town nearest to Abydos). As he then said: 'The majority of visitors, after leaving Cairo and its neighbourhood, do not make more than one or two excursions in Middle Egypt . . .'

In dismissing 350-miles' worth of Nile Valley in this seemingly cavalier manner, Weigall was not dismissing the archaeology and monuments of this long stretch, but accepting the common schedule of travellers in his day. He was himself a first-class inspector and a very good archaeological observer, if not an excavator; he wrote with a feather-light pen and was not above teasing his colleagues with sharp though unmalicious comments. It is even possible that in 1923, as archaeological correspondent of the *Daily Mail*, but denied a first-hand view of the new discovery of Tutankhamun's tomb, he perpetrated the idea of the 'curse' on the tomb, which has since perennially formed part of the whole Tutankhamun saga. When he wrote his *Guide* in 1910, Luxor was already the main goal of travellers south. Yet Middle Egypt had much to offer,

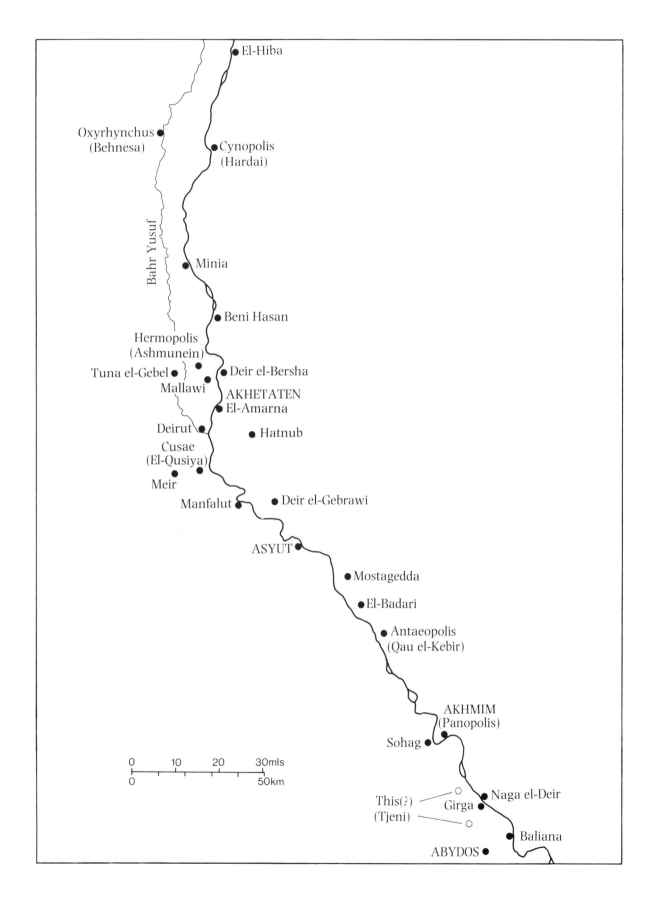

El-Hiba

Oxyrhynchus
(Behnesa)

Cynopolis
(Hardai)

Bahr Yusuf

Minia

Beni Hasan

Hermopolis
(Ashmunein)

Tuna el-Gebel

Deir el-Bersha

Mallawi

AKHETATEN
El-Amarna

Deirut

Hatnub

Cusae
(El-Qusiya)

Meir

Manfalut

Deir el-Gebrawi

ASYUT

Mostagedda

El-Badari

Antaeopolis
(Qau el-Kebir)

AKHMIM
(Panopolis)

Sohag

0    10    20    30mls
0              50km

This(?)
(Tjeni)

Girga

Naga el-Deir

Baliana

ABYDOS

Middle Egypt

perhaps even more then than today. It was, for connoisseurs of Nile travel and particularly for inquisitive Egyptologists, a very special stretch of river, to be dawdled over, to be savoured and enjoyed, and certainly not to be rushed over, to be got out of the way in anticipation of the thrills of Thebes.

It is still a very special stretch of river, and with its antiquities and its villages and small towns along the river it has a quality which induces a kind of inconsequential langour in the unsuspecting river-tourist. It is still a part of Egypt where the national inclination to put off until tomorrow what should be done today is not infrequently imposed on the traveller in a pretty conclusive way. Much of the course of the Nile is here winding and very shallow; it is a river of frequent and shifting mud-banks, where the main navigable channel changes unpredictably and demands the very special skills of the Nile pilot who can read the swirls and eddies of its sluggish stream as skilfully as a master-cook, preparing a hollandaise sauce, who reads the movements of the mixture at its various stages to prevent curdling. A moment's relaxing of attention and the sauce is beyond retrieval; equally, a moment of distraction will find the boat on a shoal and it may take hours of patient manoeuvre to work it free. Nowadays, to add to the difficulties, there is often only just enough water in the river for the navigation of boats with shallow draught, and in Middle Egypt at least, the paddle-steamer still has an advantage over a boat with a screw.

There is much evidence that the Nile has always been a river of unpredictable behaviour and of very variable course. Now that it is controlled almost to the spoonful by the High Dam, as far as water-flow is concerned, it reacts subtly in unexpected ways which are particularly evident in Middle Egypt. The high river-banks which formerly contained the Nile in flood until the water flowed over them are now being eaten away by the gentle lapping of the slow-moving stream; large sections of bank are undermined and collapse, and slowly the river extends its width, at the same time making itself shallower. Water-meadows of a fascinating kind have developed along whole stretches of the river, where cattle can graze and modest crops grow. Similar exploitation has invaded the mid-river mud-banks, now almost never submerged. Here the traveller may be obliged to contemplate a riverline and pastoral scene of timeless beauty, when life is still conducted at a pace which is governed chiefly by sunrise and sunset. Here it is good to be trapped by a mud-bank, with the knowledge that the worst that can happen is that tomorrow's excursion may be delayed, or even cancelled.

As in Weigall's day, the modern visitor usually steps off his boat in only a few places in Middle Egypt to make archaeological excursions: at Beni Hasan to see the remarkable Middle Kingdom tomb-chapels of the nomarchs of the Oryx nome; to Ashmunein with its site of Hermopolis, the city of Thoth, and its necropolis district of Tuna el-Gebel a few miles westwards on the desert edge; to El-Amarna, to visit the pathetic but remarkably evocative traces of Akhenaten's city and the neighbouring hills which contain the tombs of his supporting officials. These are the sites to be visited, their choice determined as much by the convenient schedule of the tourist boat as by their intrinsic archaeological interest. But the whole length of Middle Egypt is studded with sites worthy of a star or two (but never crossed knife and fork). It is the region of settled life, where wide plains of cultivation on the west of the Nile provide the traditional agricultural wealth and stability of the country. On the east of the Nile the rise of the land and the hills of the

Eastern Desert limit what can be done over much of the length of the river; at times very considerable hills march along with the stream, rendering the landscape even more mysterious than usual. Here were provincial centres which sustained the Egyptian state particularly during the Old Kingdom; some which came to prominence in the Middle and New Kingdoms; and during later times the region flourished, with many of the regional centres refounded as Greek cities in the Ptolemaic Period. Moments of greatness came even later, when Christianity was established in Egypt and monasticism put down some of its strongest roots in the region of modern-day Minia, Asyut, Sohag and Akhmim. One of the most striking features of the towns and villages of the region, as viewed from the river, is the common juxtaposition of mosque and church, the former marked by a crescent-crowned minaret, the latter by double towers with crosses. This region is also one where sites of some of the earliest developed prehistoric cultures in Egypt have been found. Monuments from many of these sites and from most periods have over the years entered the collections of European and American museums; they are mostly modest in size and often rather humble in character, but they illuminate corners of ancient Egyptian antiquity which are commonly overshadowed by the mighty monuments of Memphis and Thebes; they seem very suitably to represent the quiet, off-the-beaten-track quality of Middle Egypt.

Should geography or chronology determine the order in which the comprehensive, but diverse sites of Middle Egypt should be tested? There is much to be said for the geographical approach; to march (or sail) steadily up the 350 miles towards Abydos, ticking off the sites as they are passed – an Old Kingdom cemetery, an hellenised town-site, a temple, seen in substantial state in the nineteenth century but now levelled to the ground, the stones incorporated in a local sugar-factory or reduced to lime. The history and character of the region are, however, better comprehended if the chronological line is followed. A fair amount of shuffling up and down the river will be needed as period succeeds period, but in this way a far better grasp of this little-known stretch of the Nile may be gained.

The great systematic study which resulted in order being imposed on the predynastic cultures which preceded the unification of Egypt was carried out by Flinders Petrie on the basis of a large number of tombs excavated at Naqada, about twenty miles north of Luxor (about which something will be said in the next chapter). It was a pupil of Petrie, Guy Brunton, a most gifted excavator, who extended back in time the earlier limits of predynastic cultures by discoveries made especially at El-Badari and Mostagedda, two places on the east bank of the Nile, fifteen to twenty miles upstream of Asyut. The

53 The Pitt Rivers knife. The blade is of finely rippled flint with a serrated cutting edge, and the handle is of ivory carved with trails of birds and animals. A product of the Late Predynastic Period.

**54** An ivory figure of the Badarian culture: a small primitive sculpture of a woman which contains little promise of the plastic tradition which was to develop in the Dynastic Period.

inhabitants of the settlements to which the excavated cemeteries at El-Badari and Mostagedda belonged were at approximately the same stage of development as the Faiyum peoples who lived on the north shores of the Birket Qarun in the fourth millennium BC. The southerners possessed, it would seem, not only greater technological skills – they made use of copper to a small extent and discovered how to glaze soapstone – but also far stronger artistic sensibilities and inventive powers. Their pottery was of a fine, thin, red ware, usually enhanced by a carbonising process which yielded black-topped vessels. They also made human figures – indeed, they were among the first to do so in the Nile Valley.

The two best-known little figures provide extraordinary contrasts, the one with the other. Both were found at El-Badari but it is hard to believe that they represent the same cultural milieu. One is made of ivory and the other of terracotta, materials which, strangely, were not greatly used for modelling the human form during the Dynastic Period. The ivory piece is as ugly as sin, does little justice to the female form and can charitably be credited to a raw beginner (in the absence of an *avant-garde*). These comments might appear to be unjustified, levelled at an artist of a very early culture; but it will shortly be seen, when the second figure is scrutinised, that artists of exceptional ability were at work in the Badarian homeland at the same time. The ivory figure is 14 cm tall; its head is egg-shaped with eyes and mouth boldly marked, and distinguished by a huge, wide-spread nose. The body is not without lines, a waist being suggested particularly by the fuller hips rather than by a restriction of the trunk. Breasts hang pendulously, and what archaeologists are inclined to call the pubic triangle, or delta, is emphatically marked with criss-cross lines, giving the impression of an inverted triangular waffle. Limbs are poorly modelled and very sketchy. It is a piece that has in its time been much admired, but its 'primitive' quality has none of the monumental appeal of certain very early Palaeolithic figures like, for example, the so-called Venus of Willendorf or the Venus of Lespugue. It is not something that would have drawn admiration from the dynastic Egyptians.

They might, however, have derived an aesthetic thrill from the Badarian terracotta lady. Here is indeed the product of an artist who understood his material and made from it a highly successful figure. Lacking its head and the lower parts of its legs, it yet provides a remarkably seductive representation of the female form. The arms are folded just below the high, well-modelled breasts; the body is slender, but broadens substantially, although not excessively so, at the hips; a thin line running across the belly seems to be part of the modeller's intention, indicating a slight fold in the flesh. The effect of the whole is much enhanced by its excellent smooth finish; it proclaims technical competence of a very superior kind, a competence which includes first-class control in the firing of the piece.

The skills exhibited by the craftsmen of the predynastic cultures of Egypt are inevitably compared somewhat adversely with those of their successors of the First and Second Dynasties. There is a tendency to consider these early Egyptians not only predynastic but also pre-literate. It is true that the evidence for the beginnings of the hieroglyphic script before the First Dynasty is very slight, but many of the visual concepts which were later embodied in the script can be detected in the finer, decorated products of the predynastic Egyptians. These concepts, graphic indications of ways of thinking, also formed part of

**55** Men and donkeys gather on the river's edge below the tombs of Beni Hasan in the early morning, to offer their services to tourists about to disembark.

**56** Brick-making in modern Egypt. The processes used are very similar to those used in antiquity, except that modern mud-bricks are baked. The material used is ordinary Nile mud, to which chaff may be added.

the process by which the peculiar conventions of Egyptian art were developed. An excellent and instructive object in this category is a flint knife with an ivory handle which was once in the collection of General Pitt-Rivers, often described as the father of British archaeology. He acquired many Egyptian pieces, especially tools, using them for instructive comparison with implements found in the prehistoric sites which he had himself excavated. The Pitt-Rivers knife is said to have been found at Sheikh Hamada, near Sohag, and it may as a whole, or as two separate parts, have come originally from one of the many early sites in this part of Middle Egypt. Doubts about its original appearance have been raised, and there are good reasons to question its integrity as a single ancient piece. There is, however, no reason to question the authenticity of its two parts, the flint knife-blade and the carved ivory handle.

The blade itself is a masterpiece of flint-working, beautifully rippled on one side along its length, finely shaped as a cutting tool, and provided with exceptionally precise serrations along the cutting edge. It is fixed into the handle with a resinous material, but the strength of the join inspires little confidence; in use it would surely not have

53

what I wanted (for) I paid much attention to it while I was alive; and I came to it when I was grown old very happily, after I had passed my life as one among the living in the shade of my repute before the king.

There is not a great deal here to be sifted from the generalities, and Pepiankh's specific claim to have developed the necropolis area where he was buried seems difficult to justify, since his tomb is not very far from those of his predecessors. The text is inscribed on one side of the entrance to the tomb, and a second text on the other side piles up further generalities. It all looks good on paper: a very proper testimonial, an obituary written to put the best complexion on what may well have been a life and career of ups and downs. But what are we to make of this claim?

I never went to bed without having with me my seal, since I was appointed a high official. I was never put under guard; I was never restrained [? in prison]. In the matter of anything spoken against me in the presence of high officials, I emerged from it in the clear; whilst I came down upon those who spoke it, since I was cleared in it in the presence of the high officials, since they too spoke against me in maligning me.

Is there here the suggestion that at some stage in his career Pepiankh-the-Middle had been accused of some discreditable behaviour and impeached before his peers? The claims of innocence and of exoneration are sufficiently unusual to be taken seriously. Unfortunately no independent evidence can be brought to elucidate the matter. We may, however, believe his claims, for he would surely not have lived to be 100 years old and to have been buried in a fine tomb, if he had actually fallen from grace. It is nevertheless refreshing to find someone of his status even suggesting that his career had not been without stumble or hiccup. Perhaps he was more frank than most; or even so clearly crooked that an unqualified character whitewash would have been ludicrous. How then are we to take the last words of this second text? After expounding a few more of his good

58 Attendants, some of whom carry weapons, on a painted relief from the tomb of Djehutihotpe at Deir el-Bersha.

qualities and successes, he ends: 'I say so as one who speaks truthfully; I do not say so as a boaster.'

Local politics and the exercise of provincial power led at the end of the Sixth Dynasty to the disintegration of central Memphite authority and to the disorganised, unruly, pessimistic First Intermediate Period, which, together with the rise of Heracleopolis, was touched on in the last chapter. Strangely, however, the idea of developed provincial power survived this time of anarchy and re-emerged greatly strengthened in the Middle Kingdom. Fine cemeteries of nomarchs and high officials of this period are to be found throughout Middle Egypt. Of those surviving until the present day, none are finer than those at Beni Hasan, distinguished by fine architecture and a wealth of good painting. 60 The modern visitor sees them to far greater advantage than probably anyone since antiquity. For centuries the scenes have been viewed through a screen of soot and dust which has to some extent protected them from even greater vandalising than they have in any case suffered. Now systematic cleaning has brought them vividly to life and revealed much telling detail formerly unseen and unsuspected.

To visit the great tombs of Amenemhet, of the Khnumhotpes and the Bakts, nomarchs of the Sixteenth (the Oryx) nome, on the east bank of the Nile about thirty-five miles north of Meir, donkey-back was, until recently, the common way to travel. As the boat 55 approached the landing point in the early morning, as likely as not mist obscured the shore and the quiet was broken only by the plash of sounding pole and the calling of the depth of the water to the boat's captain. Then distant shouts and the drumming of little hooves announced feverish activity ashore. As the land approached, through the mist appeared a biblical scene of donkeys and donkey-boys, of self-important contractors and middlemen, many dressed in brightly coloured *galabiyas*, apart from the youngest and most miserable boys whose dress might once have been

**59** Coffin and mummy of Ankhef, from Asyut, of Eleventh Dynasty date. His face is covered with a painted cartonnage mask and his head-rest pillow stands behind his head.

**60** A scene of fig-picking, in the tomb of Khnumhotpe at Beni Hasan. Baboons join the picking party.

white. Bedlam broke out as riders and mounts were matched and bargains struck and in ten minutes or so the agitated visitor, released from his donkey would be viewing the creature's ancestors in the famous scene in the tomb of Khnumhotpe showing the arrival of trading Asiatics in the neighbourhood during the reign of Sesostris II (c. 1897–1878 BC).

At Beni Hasan, the most important tombs are cut into the cliff face overlooking the Nile, along a terrace extending from north to south nearly half a mile. In the slopes below the terrace a huge number of tombs of lesser officials, mostly of the Middle Kingdom, was excavated in 1902–4 by John Garstang of Liverpool University. Consisting of one small undecorated chamber at the bottom of a shaft, the characteristic tomb yielded rich finds of a kind typical of provincial burials of this period. The needs of the deceased were met partly by a splendid series of coffins and by models representing various activities which might form part of his posthumous environment. Such models were of special value in those tombs that lacked carved or painted scenes on their walls. The models from one tomb, belonging to a minor official called Sobkhotepi, form a representative group. There are two boats for travelling on the river, one for sailing and one for rowing. The former has a small open-sided cabin in which the owner, presumably Sobkhotepi, squats; the latter has four pairs of oarsmen. Generally speaking you travelled upstream under sail, for the prevailing wind blew south, and downstream using oars to supplement the sluggish current of the river. These boats rested on top of Sobkhotepi's coffins with a fine model granary and a model illustrating baking and brewing.

One result of the political and cultural changes that had taken place in the late Old Kingdom was the greatly increased expectations of ordinary people for their lives after death. Texts which had in the Old Kingdom been composed to help the king achieve his posthumous fate in the heavens with the sun-god Re (Pyramid Texts) were excerpted and supplemented for non-royal people and inscribed in ink on the insides of the great rectangular coffins which were used during the Middle Kingdom (Coffin Texts). Especially fine coffins were made for the provincial nobles buried in the necropolis of the Fifteenth Upper Egyptian nome (the Hare nome), at Deir el-Bersha, a few miles north of El-Amarna. The finest surviving Bersha coffin is that of Djehutinakhte in the Museum of Fine Arts, Boston, justly famous for the delicacy and richness of its paintings; but almost equally good decorations containing friezes of useful objects for the afterlife can be seen in the British Museum on the coffins of Gua, Seni and Sepi, which also preserve interesting 'maps' of the underworld. One burial of special interest is that of Ankhef, an Eleventh Dynasty official who was buried in the great cemetery of the Thirteenth Upper Egyptian nome at Asyut (in ancient times Sawty). The mummy is provided with a head-piece or mask painted with a striking representation of the face of the dead man. Such masks made of cartonnage – moulded linen stiffened with plaster – make their first appearance in the early Middle Kingdom, and as devices to establish and perpetuate the identity of the dead they stand at the beginning of a line of usage which ends 2,500 years later with the Faiyum portraits of the Roman Period.

It takes about half an hour by felucca to sail from Deir el-Bersha to El-Amarna. Here for barely twelve years was Egypt's capital, established as such by Akhenaten, a king whose record and importance are today debated unceasingly by scholars in what has become one of Egyptology's major controversial industries. First impressions on landing are unexciting unless you come filled with expectation, even a little intoxicated by the heady brew of Atenism. As likely as not, if you are an ordinary tourist visiting the place for an hour or two, you will be herded into a fiendishly uncomfortable trailer and towed behind a tractor through the village of Et-Till and across a hillocky plain, enveloped in clouds of ancient dust, incapable of concentrating on much besides holding on. After about ten minutes, which seems a good deal longer, you arrive at the cliffs and are led up to the terrace along which one group of tombs was cut for Amarna notables. From this terrace, looking westwards over the plain to the Nile, you can best gain some idea of the nature and extent of the site chosen by King Akhenaten (c. 1353–1335 BC) for his new city; an undeveloped, unpolluted area, occupying a bay or natural amphitheatre in the cliffs on the east bank of the Nile, almost equidistant from rejected Thebes and Memphis, the northern capital. Here Akhenaten could establish a new capital, a sacred city, where he and his family, supported by chosen and devoted officials, could worship the Aten, the sun-god revealed in the sun's disk. The city would be called Akhetaten, 'the Horizon of Aten'.

61 Red quartzite inlay of a face, probably from a decorative scene in the Great Temple at Akhetaten. The subject has been identified both as Akhenaten and as his successor Smenkhkare, but there are good grounds for regarding it as Nefertiti.

On a fine day one is very conscious of the sun here; there is little shade; even at the river's edge there is not much cultivation and few trees. In antiquity, no doubt, the barrenness of the site had discouraged settlers and caused it to remain undeveloped. Here temples and palaces, villas and administrative blocks, industrial and domestic areas were laid out and built in a matter of a few years, beginning possibly as early as the fourth year of the king's reign, but accelerated in pace from year six. In his seventeenth year Akhenaten died, and just as rapidly the city was abandoned and the court returned to Thebes. By the early Nineteenth Dynasty Akhetaten had been just about levelled, the stone of the temples carted across the Nile to be re-used in the buildings of Ramesses II at Khmunu, the capital city of the Fifteenth Upper Egyptian nome; the brick-built palaces and houses stripped of wood and allowed to collapse, to be covered in time by rubble and drift sand. But in this enclosed district, about eight miles from north to south and not much more than three miles deep to the eastern hills, very strange things by ancient Egyptian standards took place, and ideas were formulated, mostly in fine, elevated, poetical language, which have captured the attention and imagination of modern generations to the extent of inspiring novels, plays and even an opera. In spite of the sentimentality which distinguishes a great deal of this modern work, there is no doubt that Akhenaten, his wife Nefertiti, the romance of Akhetaten, the religious novelty of the 61 Atenist hymns and the great beauty of much Amarna art exercise a compelling 64 fascination on scholars and the general public alike.

To appreciate the spell of El-Amarna, get away from the crowd, wander alone over the bumps and depressions which once were the buildings of a fine, well-planned city, one which died suddenly and was never reoccupied or built upon again. Parts of the excavated palace and temple area can be wandered through; much has disappeared under modern cultivation. As at many ancient sites in Egypt it is here so easy to invoke the *genius loci*, but beware of over-romanticising the experience. Atenism is seductive, but rather more shallow than it is sometimes claimed to be. It is a religion of worship, of dogma, rather than one of faith and morality. But worship suits the experience of one who wanders in the early morning over these mounds and through the silted-up halls and courts of palaces and temples as the sun, the manifestation of the Aten, rises over the

62 A detail taken from the paintings on the coffin of Djehutinakhte. Various food and drink offerings to be enjoyed by the deceased are dominated by a pair of ducks with entwined necks.

eastern hills. It is not difficult to fall uncritically for Akhenaten's own words: 'You arise beautifully in the horizon of heaven, living Aten, generator of life, when you shine in the eastern horizon and fill every land with your beauty.'

Although the city of Akhetaten was abandoned and ravaged, modern excavations by British and German archaeologists have recovered much which illustrates beyond doubt the vivid splendour of the palace decorations, the luxury of many of the larger houses – bathrooms and sit-down lavatories were not uncommon – the abilities of craftsmen especially in glass and faience. Two famous heads of Nefertiti, one in Berlin and one in Cairo evoke modern standards of female beauty; many fine sculptures of members of the royal family and high officials at the court display exceptional artistic skills.

In the field of what is nowadays often, but rather dismissively, called the 'minor arts', few objects from El-Amarna can match the glass scent-bottle in the form of a fish which was found under the floor of a house in the Main City in the excavations of the Egypt Exploration Society in 1921. The body of the piece is a dark blue opaque glass into which have been worked thin rods of white and yellow glass and a little black and turquoise glass. The techniques of applying and teasing the coloured rods into ripples, chevrons and other decorative designs was brought to perfection in the Eighteenth Dynasty, and huge numbers of glass vessel fragments found at El-Amarna indicate how plentiful fine, well-formed and decorative vessels must have been in the houses of the favoured officials and of the king himself. The glass fish-bottle was surely a prized possession and it is not difficult to imagine the hope with which it may have been buried under the floor of a house by its owner, in the expectation that it might be recovered at a later date.

Another excavation find from El-Amarna inspires thoughts of a less exalted kind. It consists of two parts, made of lead, an angled pipe with a decorative bracket, and a pierced sieve terminal. These two parts when in use were connected by a hollow reed, and another reed was fitted into the other end of the angle to act as a mouthpiece. This device was used to drink beer, if the drinker was unwilling to imbibe the thick liquid with all the bits which it undoubtedly contained. Egyptian beer was made from partly baked barley bread, by fermenting the bread in water. The resulting brew, coarsely sieved, was the Egyptians' staple drink; it must often have had the consistency of thin porridge and some further device to make it more palatable was surely welcomed. There are good ancient representations of beer-drinking through such 'straws' during the New Kingdom; it may easily be thought that the caring Egyptian wife would have leapt at the chance of buying one for her husband. It may equally be thought that the robust Egyptian beer-drinker would have preferred his beer 'with body', and considered such a device a trifle namby-pamby.

There has been much scholarly debate about the possibility that Akhenaten acted as co-regent with his father, King Amenophis III, for some years and that at the time of the move to Akhetaten the old king was still alive. A little monument found in a house at El-Amarna has been used as evidence to support the co-regency theory. The scene on this little limestone stela shows Amenophis III seated with his wife Queen Tiye before a massively piled table of food offerings and blessed by the life-giving rays of the Aten. It is a strange scene, and it is made more strange by the unregal posture of the king, who is shown rather slumped in his seat. It has in fact also been used as evidence that life at the Egyptian court during the reign of Amenophis III was unusually luxurious, even

**63** Limestone relief found in a house at Akhetaten. King Amenophis III and his wife Queen Tiye sit at a table piled high with funerary offerings.

decadent. How uncritical can historians be when evidence is needed to support a thesis! It seems in general very unlikely that Panehsy, chief servitor of the Aten, one of the most important of the court officials, would have put up in his home, probably in a shrine, a stela to the living but aged father of his proper monarch, Akhenaten. There is no evidence that the old king adhered to, or even tolerated the Aten cult. But to show him in death with his wife, blessed by the rays of the Aten, would have been an entirely different matter, and a fair act of piety towards the dead father of the living king.

As we mentioned earlier, much of the stone from the Amarna temple was taken to Khmunu and used in the constructions of Ramesses II in the temple complex of the local deity Thoth, scribe of the gods, commonly represented here as a baboon. Khmunu is now known as Ashmunein, and the extensive mounds of the great city have been for some

**64** Part of a painted plaster pavement from a royal building at Akhetaten. Birds fly out of a papyrus thicket.

**65** Glass cosmetic bottle in the form of a fish, found in the Main City area of Akhetaten.

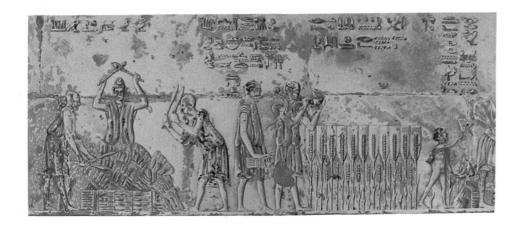

**66** A scene of harvesting and threshing barley in the tomb of Petosiris at Tuna el-Gebel. The scenes in this tomb are derived from the traditional Egyptian repertory of tomb decoration, but their design and execution show considerable Greek influence.

years the scene of British Museum excavations. So far very little has been found which throws more light on the fascinating period of transference from Akhetaten to Khmunu of huge quantities of building stone. Perhaps more than stone was transferred at that time, for discoveries made at Khmunu and possibly at its necropolis, Tuna el-Gebel, about five miles away on the desert edge, just across the Bahr Yusuf (here close to its point of departure from the Nile at Deirut), have shown that a very fine faience industry flourished here during the Twenty-first and Twenty-second Dynasties (c. 1070–712 BC). Could not the craftsmen who made such fine glass and faience at Akhetaten have transferred across the river to set up new workshops at Khmunu? Because of Thoth and his importance in the Egyptian pantheon, Khmunu was always a provincial city of more than ordinary importance, and it retained this position right down to the Graeco-Roman Period when it was given the name Hermopolis, the Greek god Hermes being equated with Thoth.

The development of agriculture which took place in Egypt during the Graeco-Roman Period led to the rapid expansion of settlement in parts of Egypt which were apparently relatively unexploited during the Pharaonic Period. The Faiyum depression, as we have seen, enjoyed the fruits of this development, and prosperity also came to Middle Egypt, abundant evidence for which can be found in the masses of written documents discovered both by chance and by excavation in the rubbish dumps of the hellenised towns of the region. If similar evidence existed for earlier periods, a very different view of provincial life in places like Khmunu and Cusae might be established. As so often, poor documentation leads to somewhat negative assessments. But the Greek papyri from Hermopolis, like those from the Greek towns in the Faiyum, provide a rich picture of life in and around these hellenised towns; apart from business, commercial and domestic papers, quantities of literary texts have been found, providing in many cases the earliest copies of the classics of Greek literature. No site has been more generous in its papyrus harvest than Oxyrhynchus, modern Behnesa, about forty miles south of Heracleopolis on the west bank of the Nile. Here enough interesting literary and non-literary documents were discovered between 1897 and 1907 to furnish material for fifty-three substantial volumes, already published, with enough still unpublished to fill an equal number. The work at Oxyrhynchus was carried out for the Egypt Exploration Fund by B.P. Grenfell and H.S. Hunt, two brilliant and indefatigable Oxford classical scholars.

67 Excavation workmen
retrieving fragments of Greek
papyrus documents from the
rubbish mound of
Oxyrhynchus.

After publication many of the texts were deposited in the Department of Manuscripts in the British Museum, which has now migrated along with the old British Museum Library to become part of the new British Library. Many more were distributed to museums and classical departments in universities throughout the world.

Oxyrhynchus, like Hermopolis, retained its importance after Christianity came to Egypt, and the whole of Middle Egypt was very receptive of the new faith. Communities of monks and anchorites were established near many of the provincial towns. The most important centre was to the west of the Nile near the modern town of Sohag, about sixty miles south of Asyut. Here, in the late fourth century, a remarkable figure in the history of Egyptian Christianity, Shenute, established a monastery which he ruled with a terrifyingly firm régime. His rules for the organisation of a monastery and for the behaviour of the inmates were influential beyond the borders of Egypt. His 'White Monastery' can still be visited – a strange fortress-like complex retaining many features of its early days and still inhabited by the daunting influence of its first abbot.

From the early Christian cemeteries in this part of Egypt, and particularly from those around the town of Akhmim on the east bank of the Nile opposite Sohag, vast quantities of so-called Coptic textiles, mostly decorated shrouds, have been taken, usually by illicit plundering. Akhmim in modern times became such a centre for trade in these textiles that examples are often described as being from Akhmim without any supporting evidence. There is something especially piquant about this rather pious reputation, for in Pharaonic times, when it was called Khent-min, Akhmim's principal local god was Min, a god of fertility, whose prominent generative member reminded the Greeks of their own somewhat disreputable Pan. For them the town became Panopolis. Among the textiles which were certainly acquired in Akhmim there are many that contain late classical imagery, sometimes wholly so, and sometimes in combination with characteristic Coptic, or at least native Egyptian, iconography. As ever, clear boundaries cannot be set.

The most remarkable textile, often described as a tapestry, was acquired in Akhmim by the Reverend Greville Chester, who presented it to the British Museum in 1889. An English clergyman of indifferent health, Chester spent most winters in Egypt and the Near East after retiring from active parish duties in 1865. He developed a fine and discriminating eye for antiquities, and supported his travels by selling part of his winter harvest of objects to museums in Britain, particularly unusual pieces which he thought to be of special interest. Such was the textile presented in 1889. As it survives, it consists of two pieces which do not quite join. The design is totally un-Egyptian, showing a pair of cupids or Erotes paddling a boat and clearly up to no good; one looks sly and determined, the other is ready for any naughtiness. The scene is bounded by an elaborate border of leaves and flowers. The two surviving corners have roundels containing masks which also radiate mischievousness; the one on the left is not a little Pan-like. The scene is carried out in coloured wools worked on a linen base and is usually dated to the third or fourth century AD.

A large linen cloth carrying decorations of a quite different style was also acquired at Akhmim, and may have originated in one of the cemeteries in the neighbourhood. It is probably a century or more later in date than that with the boating cupids, and its decorations are distinctly hybrid. The design is again executed in coloured wools on a plain linen backing; its principal components are two figures set in panels divided and flanked by elaborate bands containing dancing male and female figures, with intertwining vine tendrils and formalised patterns based on floral and geometrical designs. The large female figure in the right-hand panel holds a bow and arrow and has three more arrows in a quiver on her back; she is thought to be Artemis (Diana), the huntress. Her companion in the left-hand panel is less clearly identified; he wears a Phrygian cap and leans on his reversed spear; by analogy he should also be a hunter, perhaps Actaeon or Orion, or even Meleager. No matter whom the principal figures represent, they are without a doubt drawn from the pagan ranks of classical mythology; but the manner of representation of the figures, and the general layout of the textile's decorative scheme are more than suggestive of what may be called Coptic. There is nothing identifiably Christian in the motifs, but the hands of Egyptian designers and

**68** Textile fragments from Akhmim, usually described as tapestry, showing cupids or Erotes paddling a boat.

craftsmen can be distinguished here – people who may already have been converted to Christianity, or would shortly be so. Here again to distinguish which strain in the Egyptian population contributed what element to a design of this kind is quite impossible, and indeed quite otiose. So would the process of mixing continue after the Islamic conquest in the seventh century. What may be identified unequivocally as Islamic in matters of design can easily be accepted as such; but other influences – native Egyptian, Byzantine Egyptian – continue to exist, to be intermingled, to absorb. What is not distinctly Islamic tends to be called Coptic, whether it shows Christian symbolism or not. Coptic is a word loaded with religious and linguistic connotations; in a sense, and certainly for the second half of the first millenium AD, and probably for several more centuries, it means native Egyptian. And Middle Egypt was its very solid base.

# CHAPTER FIVE

# The Holy Place

## ABYDOS

THE FEELING of awe which some people experience when they visit El-Amarna is by no means unique. Shrines, places of pilgrimage, the houses of great authors, composers and thinkers, all inspire the properly attuned visitor with suitable *frissons*. You commonly need to know something about the place and its peculiar associations before the local 'vibrations' can be picked up, and the hair rise, even the flesh creep. Sympathetic feelings also help. Abydos is a place that can affect a visitor even if he comes with no expectations, no knowledge and no sympathy. It is unquestionably one of the most numinous places in Egypt – to walk about its monuments and mounds is to experience strong feelings of what might be recognised as a spiritual presence. Indeed you may even meet the deity.

If you walk northwards from the great temples of Sethos I and Ramesses II and then go left towards the hills of the Western Desert, or half-left in the direction of the Shunet ez-Zebib, you will soon find yourself in a barren waste of little hills and dips, the ground littered with broken pots, fragments of linen cloth, bones; the remains of unbaked

69 View over the desert at Abydos, looking west from the Terrace of the Great God towards Poqer.

mud-brick walls announce the presence of a wide-spread network of buildings, once excavated and now partly buried under rubble and drift sand. Keep your eyes skinned, and as likely as not you will raise a fox-like animal which will not wait to be identified; it will be off towards the hills or even down towards the palm-lined fringe of the cultivation. You will have seen Khentiamentiu, the most ancient of the local gods of Abydos.

It is a special thrill to find the antique magic of the autochthonous form of divinity still making itself felt through the proper appearance of the god in his ancient and recognisable form. In Egypt, where in antiquity the presence of god was to be found in a wide variety of creatures and natural phenomena, there remain places today where the ancient form of the deity still reveals itself in unmistakable manner. The sun, of course, almost always to be seen, especially in Upper Egypt, is the most obvious example; its recognition as the clearest manifestation of divinity put Re at the head of the Egyptian pantheon, reinterpreted with subtle undertones as the Aten in the time of Akhenaten and Nefertiti. But the sun, for our purpose, is too universal; it is not local and particular. At Edfu, however, stand in front of the great temple pylon and it will not be long before a falcon soars into view – Horus the Behdetite, Horus of Edfu, the local god himself. Wander about in the scrubby neighbourhood of the mounds of Buto in the Delta and you may well encounter – less amusingly – Wadjet or Edjo, the 'Lady of Pe and Dep, foremost in Buto', the cobra, tutelary deity of Pharaoh as king of Lower Egypt.

To meet Khentiamentiu at Abydos is special, however. It is just right that he should be seen rushing about the desert range, and especially so if he makes towards the hills and to the area where kings of the first two dynasties were buried, and where by legend the

The sacred area at Abydos.

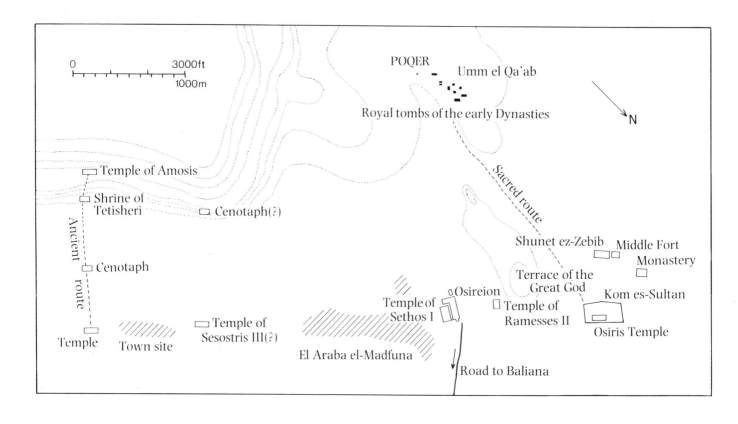

grave of Osiris is located. By name Khentiamentiu was 'Foremost of the Westerners', i.e. first among the blessed dead, who in death travelled to the West. There in due course was established the realm of Osiris, the mythical martyred king of Egypt, who himself became 'Foremost of the Westerners'. So the local canine deity, fox, jackal, or hybrid, became assimilated into the cycle of Osiris legends and from the time of the Old Kingdom ceased to be seen as a separate deity. But dog-like deities continued to be attracted to Abydos, to take up, as it were, the watch-dog functions and mortuary duties of Khentiamentiu. There was, most importantly, Anubis, the embalming deity above all others, whose local base was Hardai in the Seventeenth Upper Egyptian nome – known to the Greeks as Cynopolis (Dog-city); there was also Wepwawet, 'Opener of the ways', divine dispatch-rider, running wildly with the messages of the gods – his home originally was Sawty, modern Asyut, ninety miles north of Abydos.

The bewildering chopping and changing that went on within the varied and complex community of Egyptian deities can only be understood if it is accepted that ordinary rationality does not apply. Many associations between the gods of different places were the result of political changes and regroupings. At Abydos, the cause of the many changes that took place during the first millennium of the Dynastic Period was the rise of the cult of Osiris and the association of the god with Abydos, the site of his tomb. Something more of the development of the cult will emerge later in this chapter. For the moment, let us consider Abydos as a centre of pilgrimage, a place for periodic festivals, not unlike the shrines of European Christendom at times of the great mystic celebrations of the Christian year, and particularly those places where in Holy Week the events of Jesus' last hours are re-enacted in public procession with much scourging and flagellation. An account of one series of religious pageants is recorded by a royal treasurer, Iykhernofret, who was sent to Abydos by King Sesostris III (c. 1878–1841 BC) of the Twelfth Dynasty on the occasion of one year's Osiris festival, to supervise the arrangements:

My majesty orders that you are instructed to go up-stream to Abydos in the Thinite (Eighth) nome to make the monument of his father Osiris, Foremost of the Westerners (Khentiamentiu), to embellish his secret image with the fine gold which he let my Majesty bring from Nubia in triumph and justification . . . Now my Majesty sent you to do this because my Majesty knew that no one else but you could do it. Set off, and come back when you have done everything that my Majesty has ordered.

I did everything his Majesty ordered, putting into effect what my Lord ordered for his father Osiris, Foremost of the Westerners . . . I acted as royal deputy for Osiris, Foremost of the Westerners; I embellished his great barque of eternity and everlasting . . .

He then describes other arrangements he made and the preparation of the *neshmet*-barque, Osiris' special craft, and continues:

I organised the going-forth of Wepwawet when he proceeds to protect his father. I drove back the enemies from the *neshmet*-barque; I felled the enemies of Osiris, I organised the great going-forth, following the god in his steps . . . I equipped him in his fine regalia when he proceeded to the district of Poqer. I made clear the path of the god to his tomb before Poqer. I protected Onnophris [Osiris] on that day of great struggle; I felled all his enemies on the sand-bank(?) of Nedyt. I caused him to go up into the great barque; it displayed his beauty. I delighted the eastern desert; I made rejoicing

71 Wooden model funerary boat, placed in a burial to act magically as a substitute for the journey of pilgrimage to Abydos by the mummy of the deceased.

in the western desert. They saw the beauty of the *neshmet*-barque when it reached land at Abydos, when it delivered Osiris, Foremost of the Westeners, Lord of Abydos, to his palace . . .

This interesting text, on a limestone stela in Berlin, provides a rare glimpse – inevitably too fleeting – of the kind of religious mystery-play which was certainly enacted at most of the important shrines throughout Egypt during antiquity. Ideally the king would attend, but almost invariably he would be represented by a deputy as here at Abydos in the person of Iykhernofret. The fate of Osiris was the central event in the pageant; but in the early stages, attacked by his enemies – surely the followers of his brother, the malevolent Seth – he is protected by Wepwawet, the successor of Khentiamentiu who himself is now wholly assimilated into the person of Osiris. The procession to Osiris' tomb probably followed a way leading from the most ancient Osiris temple at the northern end of the divine region of Abydos, over the desert to the place called Poqer, a distance of about a mile. It is not difficult to visualise the events: the god in his barque, attacked by enemies who are routed by Wepwawet, impersonated no doubt by a man wearing a dog/jackal mask, rushing around barking and snapping at those who dare to assault Osiris. When Osiris reaches his tomb in Poqer he has effectively fulfilled his destiny, and can return to his temple in triumph and joy.

69

Although the evidence is thin, enough inscriptional and archaeological material has been found at Abydos to indicate that its hey-day in popular terms was the Middle Kingdom, the Twelfth and early Thirteenth Dynasties. This conclusion may surprise those who know Abydos as the site firstly of the great temple of Sethos I, and secondly of the smaller, but charming, temple of his son Ramesses II. A visit to the older great collections of Egyptian antiquities – Berlin, Leiden, London, Paris, Turin – will quickly reveal the existence of hundreds of stelae (inscribed stone tablets), offering-tables and sculptures which are known, or reasonably believed, to have come from Abydos. As many again can be seen in the Cairo Museum. A very great number of these memorial pieces, perhaps even the majority, came not from tombs but from dummy tombs or cenotaphs sited in the Abydos necropolis so that the person commemorated might be close to Osiris in his most holy place and even participate in the offerings presented to the god.

70 The edge of the cultivation with palm trees, on the east side of the sacred district of Abydos.

73 *(left)* Limestone block statue of Sihathor, placed in a niche stela and originally part of Sihathor's cenotaph at Abydos.

74 *(above)* Ivory tablet originally attached by a cord to a receptacle possibly containing a pair of sandals. King Den smites an Asiatic.

75 *(right)* Ivory figure of an Early-Dynastic king, found in the Osiris Temple at Abydos. The short cloak is a characteristic part of the king's equipment for the *Sed*-festival.

immediately from the main mass. It is as if the subject has been squashed into a compact block. And yet here, as commonly in block-statues of later date, the feeling conveyed is not one of tension, but one of repose. It is a peculiarly Egyptian sculptural form, of which this Sihathor is one of the earliest, and indeed one of the best. Block-statues of the New Kingdom and Late Period are often treated principally as vehicles for inscription, the broad surfaces providing excellent spaces for wordy texts. Sihathor has been spared this over-writing. Two lines of text down the front between the legs are quite enough, because the appropriate texts can be found on the false-door stela which houses his statue. For the rest, the figure is splendidly carved; the artist has quickly appreciated the subtle sculptural advantage to be extracted from the form, suggesting well-shaped limbs beneath the enveloping cloak. And so Sihathor squats cosily in his niche, awaiting eternity in close proximity to his god Osiris.

Let us tarry a little longer at this northern end of the Abydos holy precinct, to survey what else may be seen and to consider the importance of the place in earlier times. If the processional route is traced, the way begins close to the cultivation where the earliest temple of Osiris has been identified as the spot now called Kom es-Sultan; in the other direction, to the west, the way leads to Poqer – an area close to the desert hills which is known locally as Umm el-Qa'ab, 'Mother of pots', because the ground there is littered thickly with pot-sherds. Both temple and pot-sherd area have produced remarkable finds in excavations, although there is now very little to be seen in either place apart from remains of mud-brick walls which defy casual interpretation. In both sites Flinders Petrie made surprising discoveries which at the time had profound implications for the early history of the Dynastic Period.

Two ivory royal figures were recovered from the Osiris precinct. One, which is now in the Cairo Museum, shows King Cheops, builder of the Great Pyramid, seated on a simple block throne with low back, holding in his right hand the royal flail and wearing the red crown of Lower Egypt. The identification is certain because the king's name is carved on the front of the throne. The face is remarkably strong, and conveys vividly an impression of a monarch who exercised absolute power. The impression gained from the second ivory figure is altogether different. Here we see a far less determined characterisation – a king entering into the performance of a solemn ceremony. Apart from the loss of the legs and base, the little figure is mostly intact. It portrays a king, wearing the white crown of Upper Egypt, and a short cloak which is clearly decorated with a lozenge pattern. This is the cloak worn in certain of the ceremonies of the *Sed*-festival, an occasion of great importance in the reign of an Egyptian king. It took place on the thirtieth anniversary of his coronation and was in essence a festival of renewal in which his power was revived and the king in a sense revivified and rededicated to his royal and divine purposes. In the Old Kingdom and later, the *Sed*-festival was celebrated in Memphis, and its news of hope and renewal was conveyed by royal messenger to all the provincial capitals. What purpose was served by this statuette is unknown. The deposit in which it was found was dated by Petrie to the first two dynasties, and in spite of objections, both serious and frivolous, there remains very good reason for retaining his dating. Abydos was without a doubt a place of great royal importance in the early dynasties, and it is not beyond the limits of good argument to suggest that some part of the renewal festival may have been celebrated there. But considering the figure as it stands, you can see, in miniature, a

75

thought-provoking representation of monarchy, not strong and absolute, like the little ivory Cheops, but somewhat withdrawn, reticent even, showing perhaps the weight of royal responsibility. The whole piece is very delicately carved, and the lines of the face in particular are very sensitively portrayed. Here is a king stepping forward to renew his vows and his responsibilities, weighed down by his heavy quilted cloak, and perhaps by the contemplation of thirty years of power.

At Poqer, the western terminal of the processional way was, according to Egyptian 'historical' belief, the tomb of Osiris. In fact Poqer was the burial-place of most of the kings of the First and Second Dynasties. There are some scholars (but perhaps not now as many as a few years ago) who would dispute this statement, believing that the real burial-places of the Early Dynastic kings were at Saqqara, and that the Abydos tomb-like structures are kinds of dummy tombs, even cenotaphs. The debate may not be over yet; it certainly cannot easily be settled by existing evidence. What is certain, however, is that these funerary monuments were discovered in the late nineteenth century by the French archaeologist Emile Amélineau, and were, a few years later, re-excavated by Petrie. Finds were mostly small and fragmentary, the pitiful left-overs of repeated ransackings in antiquity. Enough was found to establish the identity of the early kings; there was a rich, if unspectacular, harvest of potentially important historical documents. One which establishes the character of the early monarchy as being recognisably from an Egyptian mould, which would be remodelled constantly for the subsequent 3,000 years, is a small ivory rectangular plaque or label. It has a small hole in one corner, indicating that it was probably tied by a cord to some container; and on one side are scratched the outlines of a pair of sandals. Reasonably it may be described as the label attached to a box containing sandals. The other side of the label, however, carries the startling scene of a king laying into a kneeling, almost recumbent, figure of a man, with a heavy mace.

The king is identified by the signs written in the rectangle surmounted by a falcon. He is Den, or Udimu, the fourth or fifth ruler of the First Dynasty, and his enemy, identified by quite distinctive facial features, including the beard and the Semitic nose, represents some Asiatic tribe or nation. The signs on the right are usually read as 'the first occasion of smiting the East' and taken as indicating some punitive strike against Asiatics, either in the eastern region of the Delta or even in south-western Palestine. There is much in this tiny scene which relates to the symbolism of the Egyptian monarch in later periods, in the way the king is equipped, for instance with the bull's tail which figures regularly in later ritualistic scenes. He also sports on his head-band the uraeus – the sacred serpent of Edjo or Wadjet of Lower Egypt, who protected the king as the Lower Egyptian monarch. The scene is one of the earliest-known examples of the king smiting his enemies, a common representation found as late as the Graeco-Roman Period, when it was carved in colossal size on the outer faces of temple pylons. The standard behind the smitten enemy supports a dog/jackal deity and a strange balloon-like object. This in later times would be Wepwawet, but at this early period it may still be Khentiamentiu. One further very interesting detail is that the ground-line on which the king and captive stand rises sharply on the right and is marked with dots in a manner found very much later in Egyptian art to represent the stony, hilly desert.

In recent years new excavations in the area of the royal tombs have been undertaken by the German Archaeological Insititute. Modern methods have already shown that

76 The excavations of Flinders Petrie at Abydos: work on the clearance of the burial chamber in the tomb of King Den.

there is more to be discovered in this important place, and it cannot be doubted that some well-established views will need considerable revision in due course.

Nearer the cultivation and the early temple, and further to the north of the processional way and the area known as the Terrace of the Great God, are the striking and substantial ruins of a huge mud-brick enclosure, with the less evident remains of others near by. This is known as the Shunet ez-Zebib, 'storeroom of dates', and after a century of study and excavation it remains enigmatic. It broods over its district, glowering and mysterious, with double walls and protected entrances, massive and presumably impregnable in its time. There has been much debate also over its date, although most scholars would now place it in the Early Dynastic Period. The idea that it

78

77 Conglomerate statue of Khaemwese, high-priest of Ptah and for a time crown-prince of Ramesses II. The nature of the standards he carries here suggests an Abydos origin for the sculpture.

and the others close by were fortresses or great stores is now generally discounted, and the favoured view is that they were probably the remains of funerary temples or cenotaphs associated with the royal tombs at Poqer.

Why was this place chosen for so many important structures, including royal tombs, in the time of the earliest dynasties? Somewhere near by was the city and nome capital known in remote antiquity as Tjeni and by the Greeks as This, the site of which has never been established with certainty. It may have been in the neighbourhood of the modern town of Girga about twelve miles to the north. Traditionally the kings of the First and Second Dynasties are known as Thinite, and it must be supposed that, for reasons wholly unknown, their original seat of power was in this region. Abydos might be thought to be rather far from Girga to serve as the royal burial ground, but the local association with the god Khentiamentiu may have provided the clinching argument. The ancient name of this chosen place was Abdju, turned into Abydos by the Greeks, reminded no doubt, of the Greek city of the same name in the Hellespont.

The whole of the Abydos region must have been charged with activity in the centuries leading up to the triumph of the Thinite kings. As we shall learn in a later chapter, many of the most significant sites of predynastic Egypt have been excavated in the stretch of the Nile Valley between Abydos and Thebes, and at El-Amra, six miles to the south, the contents of the early predynastic graves were so abundant and characteristic that Petrie chose to call this early stage of Egyptian culture Amratian. From this general area are said to come two very remarkable slate, or schist, objects which are usually called ceremonial palettes. The slate palettes found in early tombs were clearly used for the grinding of eye-paint – the necessary salve applied to the eyes for therapeutic and cosmetic reasons. Malachite (green) and galena (black) were both used, and traces have been found on these slate palettes, which were often in the shape of animals, birds, fish and reptiles. Ceremonial palettes, so-called, are much grander, the biggest and most famous being that in the Cairo Museum ascribed to King Narmer, who may have been the uniter of Upper and Lower Egypt. It was found at Hieraconpolis much further to the south. The palettes from the Abydos region are smaller, but carved with exceptionally interesting and intriguing low-relief scenes which have stimulated much speculation.

The larger of the two, as now surviving, consists of three fragments making up over ninety per cent of the original whole. A cast of the part in the Louvre is exhibited with the two parts in the British Museum. A reminder of its origin as a cosmetic object is provided by an undecorated circular area surrounded by a raised lip – the putative grinding point; but there are no signs that eye-paint was ever ground here, even for the most formal or ceremonial reasons. For the purpose of this palette is to act as a vehicle for a series of low-relief carvings which fills the remainder of the principal surface; the other side is smooth and undecorated. The theme of the decoration is, on the simplest level, taken to be the hunting of wild animals, and for this reason the object is commonly known as the 'Hunters' Palette'. Armed men – the hunters – are ranged round the edge of the surface and wild animals occupy the centre of the field. The hunters, so-called, are elaborately armed with spears, bows and arrows, maces, throw sticks (perhaps with the properties of the boomerang) and ropes; some carry standards which incorporate images of recognisable deities (falcons) and divine symbols, the marks of tribes or regions and possibly the forerunners of nome-standards. Among the animals, which include various

78 (top) The fortified enclosure of the Shunet ez-Zebib at Abydos.

79 (above) A group of pottery vessels from predynastic burials. The box-shaped container decorated with antelopes comes from the cemetery at El-Amra, a little to the south of Abydos.

80 (right) Painted limestone relief of the god Thoth from the Temple of Ramesses II at Abydos. This ibis-headed deity was considered to be the secretary of the gods, and here he is shown carrying a scribe's palette.

The Hunters' Palette. Armed men surround animals of various kinds, the most noticeable being the great lion on the right, possibly representing the defeated chieftain of the enemy.

horned species of the antelope and deer families, hares, dogs or jackals, ostrich and hartebeest, the most prominent are two lions, which have been the principal object of attack. Here is a scheme of decoration full of hidden meaning. It cannot be believed that the scene is simply a representation of a rather important hunt; reference to internal feuds and squabbles of the kind which are generally thought to have preceded the unification of Egypt have been suggested, and it seems impossible to avoid some interpretation along this line. But to disentangle with any precision exactly what each element and detail may represent is the task of the higher speculator in historic interpretation. It is enough to admire on a simple level the vitality and interest of this early relief and to see in it so much that can be related to the better-understood work of dynastic times.

Similar doubts attend the interpretation of the scenes on the second great palette 82 which may also have come from the Abydos region. Again the surviving fragments are scattered through three collections (the British Museum has the lower half; the Ashmolean Museum the large upper part, and the third, small, fragment is in a Swiss private collection); there are low-relief carvings on both sides. The principal scene, on the side we may call the recto, incorporates, as in the case of the 'Hunters' Palette', the circular grinding area, again contained within a raised rim. Dominating the scene is a lion on the rampage, savaging a man, one of several who lie in various positions of discomfort (one has his arms bound together), prey to the attacks of carrion birds – vultures and ravens. Part of a bound captive can be seen at the top right; he stands in front of a person wearing a long garment decorated with a simple 'eye' motif. Two further captives, smaller in scale, are shown on the left of the upper fragment; they are gripped tightly by arms emerging from standards bearing images of the falcon and ibis. Other fallen victims or captives were clearly depicted in the missing top part of the recto. The symbolism of this scene has suggested a bloody encounter, again possibly an incident in the struggle for unification, if not the representation of that important episode as a whole. It is therefore known as the 'Battlefield Palette', and the lion is perhaps the symbolic victor of the struggle. Who can tell? No help comes from our examination of the scene on the verso. Here are two long-legged, long-necked, animals grazing off the fronds of a palm-tree. They should, one feels, be giraffes, but experts have ruled out such an identification; we must settle for gerenuk, a kind of antelope, but nobody is very satisfied with this zoological diagnosis. A plump fowl-like bird occupies the field behind the head of one of the tall creatures – possibly a guinea-fowl. There is even less of obvious significance in this verso scene to allow a reasonable interpretation. Speculative explanations – for example, Upper and Lower Egypt feeding together placidly in the unified land represented by the palm-tree – are so fanciful that they may be right. It is simpler to enjoy this scene, and indeed that most explicit recto scene, as remarkable early manifestations of Egyptian artistic skills.

Visitors to Abydos today come principally to see the great temple inaugurated by King Sethos I of the Nineteenth Dynasty and completed by his son Ramesses II. For this temple alone the daunting journey from Baliana, the nearest town on the Nile, is more than worth attempting. The ancient site lies a little more than six miles west of the town, and the straight narrow road, raised on a dyke and bounded by a small canal on the north side and by an unreasonable drop to the cultivated fields on the south, is the race-track for taxi-drivers who see Abydos as the turning point of a long chariot-course. Out with

82 The Battlefield Palette. The lion, probably representing the king, seizes his enemies.

83 Painted relief from the great Osiris temple of King Sethos I at Abydos. The king offers a platter of food to Isis, 'mother of the god'.

one load of expectant tourists; then back with a load of demoralised ones, as quickly as possible, so as not to miss the next batch of eager expectants. If the road were wider, if the verges were reliable, if there were no other taxis, or camels loaded with sugar-cane, or groups of dignitaries on donkeys, or little carts crammed with ladies dressed wholly in black and off to market, then the journey might be less hazardous. God is usually merciful, but it is trying to have one's own natural caution overridden by the confident fatalism of the local Jehu.

At the end of the road, and quite unexpectedly, for there survive no mighty pylons or obelisks to mark the presence of a great temple, lies one of the most inspiring and beautiful structures in the whole of Egypt. Sethos' temple stands close by the modern village of El-Araba el-Madfuna, home for many years of Dorothy Eady, known locally and to two generations of tourists as Umm Seti, 'Mother of Seti (Sethos)'. She was in effect the self-appointed mistress of the Abydos temple in modern times, recognised as such by the Egyptian Antiquities Organization, the guardian of the ancient rituals, slightly possessed, and no mean Egyptologist although a little disorganised. She, more than anyone, impressed visitors with the special qualities of Abydos, and of her temple in particular. She always took off her sandals on entering the sacred precinct, and her evident piety never seemed out of place.

Umm Seti's temple of Sethos I was not quite the same in conception and purpose as that recognised as normal by Egyptologists. It is in any case a strange temple by Egyptian standards. It is not a cult-temple in the ordinary sense, and it is not a funerary temple. Shrines to many deities are to be found in its many chapels, and there is great emphasis on those gods whose functions were concerned with death, resurrection and the necropolis, and especially Osiris. The cult of the dead royal ancestors was included in the ceremonies celebrated in the temple, and one of the most notable scenes, so awkwardly placed in a narrow corridor that it defies easy photography, shows Sethos with the young Ramesses about to honour all their royal predecessors, starting with Menes the unifier of Egypt. The names of the ancestor kings are placed in tabulation before Sethos and his son as if they were set down in writing on papyrus. The list is by no means complete; there are large gaps for the difficult periods of Egyptian history when unity was tenuous or non-existent. Similarly, Akhenaten, of hated memory, and his successors, tainted somewhat by the same stain, are eliminated, although their reigns fall within the preceding century.

Sethos' temple is noted especially for the purity and beauty of the limestone reliefs in the parts of the temple completed while he still lived. Many scenes retain much of their original paint; but although the colour is striking and of very great interest, the connoisseur cannot fail to prefer those scenes where the paint is lost, and the stunning quality of the low reliefs can be appreciated without distraction of colour. A great part of the temple, however, was completed in the reign of Ramesses II, and the work here is heavy and generally undistinguished from an artistic point of view. It is strange that this should be so – if we may for the moment forget the indifferent quality of much of the multitudinous work carried out elsewhere in Ramesses' reign – for not half a mile away to the north Ramesses had his own multicultic temple constructed, a delicate, lightly decorated, unponderous, small-scale shrine, where the finely carved, brightly painted reliefs delight and surprise visitors. This can hardly be the work of Ramesses the Great, the mighty builder; but so it is. The explanation may well be that when he assumed responsibility for the completion of his father's temple, he transferred the skilled work-men who had already shown their worth to construct his own, leaving the completion of the earlier temple to less experienced – certainly less competent – craftsmen.

It is, of course, unlikely that Ramesses himself had much to do with these operations at Abydos, but we may believe that the hand of his son Khaemwese may be detected. In Chapter 2 on Memphis, where this great royal official was discussed, mention was made of a statue thought to have come originally from Abydos. It is a remarkable carving, a test of the most able stone-worker's skill. The material is deceptive. It is clear that the craftsman who selected the stone initially must have been attracted by its remarkable colour, a rich brown with areas of honey-yellow which might be exploited in the final carving. Unfortunately, the surface disguised pockets of pebble-rich conglomerate which were exposed as the piece was reduced to shape. These pebbles proved almost impossible to carve, and many had to be prised out of their beds, leaving disfiguring holes which were presumably filled with a patching plaster. Even so, the sculptor succeeded in producing an extraordinarily fine piece which is mostly impeccably carved; but in places – for example the torso, from left shoulder to right hip – the pebble texture is very apparent and gives the statue a strange leprous aspect. The head, fortunately, is almost perfect, and it presents a noble, handsome, impression of the great Khaemwese.

When first discovered in modern times, this statue was in private hands in the neighbourhood of Asyut; but it has long been thought probable that it stood at one time in Abydos, possibly in the Sethos temple or in the neighbouring Ramesses shrine. Two standards held in Khaemwese's hands suggest Abydos strongly. One is topped by a strange wig-like fetish embellished with two uraei or royal serpents; this object is closely associated with the Osiris cult at Abydos. The second standard was originally surmounted by three divine figures, most surely to be identified as the divine triad of Abydos, Osiris, Isis and Horus. The association with Abydos is confirmed by the contents of the texts on the statue, in which, among other things, Khaemwese associates himself closely with Osiris, points out the great works he has carried out for him and on behalf of his father Ramesses II, and established for himself a qualification to participate in the royal offerings to the great god.

It is not possible to say whether the occasion for Khaemwese's activities at Abydos, so far away from Memphis, took place early or late in the reign of his father. Probability requires a date somewhat advanced into the reign, because the prince could scarcely have been born when his father acceded to the throne. But work on the Ramesses temples at Abydos must have lasted for many years and Khaemwese's contributions could have come towards the completion of the major operations. All this, however, is pure speculation. Even more speculative is the suggestion that Khaemwese may have inspired the setting up of a king-list in the small temple of Ramesses II. Undoubtedly modelled on the list in the Sethos temple, this second version has been less generously treated by time and the hand of man. It was already very considerably damaged when it was first discovered in 1818 by the enterprising William John Bankes of Kingston Lacy in Dorset, whose travels in the Mediterranean and the Near East were inspired as much by the need to absent himself from England as by a genuine interest in art and archaeology. His place in the early history of Egyptology is assured not only for his actual discoveries,

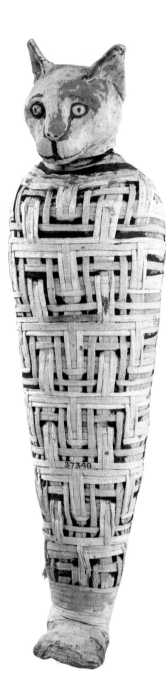

but also for some very real contributions to the early history of hieroglyphic decipherment and to the identification of significant monuments. The king-list of Ramesses II was one such monument, and through good copies he made it known to a wide scholarly acquaintance. His restraint in leaving this valuable historical document in position in the temple was not matched by equal respect from Jean François Mimaut, the French Consul-General, who had it removed to his personal collection in 1829. Ultimately, but by then irrevocably divorced from the parent monument, the king-list was purchased from Mimaut's estate and brought to London in 1839.

In its much damaged condition, this king-list preserves in whole or in part the names of only thirty-four ancestor kings, mostly of the Sixth and Seventh Dynasties, the Twelfth Dynasty and the Eighteenth and Nineteenth Dynasties. The list is again very selective, and it is certain that its purpose was not to provide an historical record of all the previous rulers of Upper and Lower Egypt, but rather to enumerate those who, for various reasons, were considered worthy of memorialising and of receiving offerings. Certain exceptions can easily be comprehended – the Hyksos rulers, and again the Amarna Pharaohs. But why should kings of the Seventh Dynasty be so favoured by inclusion? There seems to be no reasonable explanation; but it is not unreasonable to wonder whether some names were included simply to make up numbers, after the great and obligatory names of the founding fathers, of the great rulers of the Old and Middle Kingdoms, and of the immediate and acceptable predecessors of the Eighteenth and Nineteenth Dynasties had been selected.

The king-lists, like so much else at Abydos, proclaim the supreme royal attachment to the place, one which began with the burials of the kings of the first two dynasties but which developed through the association of the site with Osiris, the divine martyr-king of legend. A more comprehensive survey of the whole archaeological field would have drawn attention to the many royal monuments which lie to the west and south of the great Sethos temple. They have mostly been identified as cenotaphs – dummy or secondary burial-places – where the great kings, whose true posthumous fate lay in the company of the sun-god Re, might acquire a secondary, more intimate, association with Osiris, the great king of the underworld. These monuments can now scarcely be identified, so little remains to be seen. But it is not true of the strange, massively constructed, subterranean building known as the Osireion. This, apparently another cenotaph, started by Sethos I and completed by Merenptah, successor of Ramesses II, has in its central and most sacred part no inscriptions, and it seems to reproduce conceptually the burial of Osiris himself. The huge monolithic granite 'sarcophagus', lapped about by stagnant green water, softened by a lush growth of adventitious vegetation, may be observed from above, from the edge of what seems to be a great industrial crater. It should be a place of awe and wonderment, but the bright sun of Egypt and a kind of builder's-yard ambience brought about by too much abandoned archaeological equipment and the local hopefuls who loaf about, snapping at the periphery of tourist groups, diminish the atmosphere disastrously. The Osireion can be the subject of an interesting visit, and it can induce feelings of mystery and holiness in the receptive visitor. But for the true magic of Abydos walk the moon-landscape between the Ramesses temple and the Shunet ez-Zebib. Here you may feel the power of the place, and here, if you are lucky, you may see Khentiamentiu.

**84** (*left*) Part of the king-list from the temple of Ramesses II at Abydos. Shadowy kings of the Seventh Dynasty are named in the top row; great kings of the Eighteenth Dynasty in the middle row; Ramesses II's cartouches alternate for the whole bottom row.

**85** Mummy of a cat from the animal cemeteries at Abydos.

# CHAPTER SIX
# City of Temples
# EASTERN THEBES

SOMETIME IN the early second millennium BC the god Amun hijacked the town of Wese from the god Month (Montju, Mentu). It happened early in the Twelfth Dynasty, but the reason for this local religious revolution has never been satisfactorily determined. Month was a falcon-headed deity with warlike propensities, and was primarily the god of the Fourth nome of Upper Egypt, the capital city of which was originally Armant, a name quite clearly derived from the ancient Iun-Montju. Armant lies on the west bank of the Nile just a few miles to the south of Luxor, and it lost its importance to the Theban district during the Eleventh Dynasty, when the ruling line (formerly the nomarchs of the region) chose to construct tombs and funerary temples on the west bank of Thebes.

Private letters of the late Eleventh Dynasty, some of which were excavated at Thebes and were certainly written in the neighbourhood, contain greetings which invoke Month, Lord of Wese. Nehesi, described as a general, writes to Kay: 'How are you, how are you? Are you alive, prosperous and healthy? Your condition is like living a million times. May Month, Lord of Wese, and all the gods, help you! May they make for you a million years of life, prosperity and health . . . just as I wish!' In later times, precedence in greeting was given to Amun or Amon-Re. A letter of the Eighteenth Dynasty, from Hori to Ahmose contains the greeting: 'in the favour of Amon-Re, King of the Gods, of Ptah, South-of-his-wall, of Thoth, Lord of the god's word, and of all the gods and goddesses who are in Karnak.' Ahmose, in fact, had supervisory duties which took him to Armant, although, again, it is probable that this letter, like others in his small surviving archive, came from Thebes.

Amun was a strange faceless god in origin, one of the company of gods which was based at Khmunu (Hermopolis) in Middle Egypt. He was the 'hidden one', whose name in the hieroglyphic script was sometimes 'determined' (that is, qualified by what is usually a helpful, explicatory sign) by an empty space; the 'hidden one' could not be satisfactorily 'determined'. For some reason his cult commended itself to the kings of the Twelfth Dynasty, and although they transferred their capital to Itj-tawy, hundreds of miles away to the north, near the entrance to the Faiyum depression, they established a sanctuary to Amun at Wese, on the east bank, certainly in the area now occupied by the great temple of Karnak. In time Amun became closely associated with other gods; first and foremost with Re, as Amon-Re, dignified as King of the Gods, a universal deity and in time the god of Egyptian empire; also with Min, the fertility deity of Coptos, about thirty miles north of Thebes, in which identification he is commonly shown with a prominent male member.

What happened at Wese/Thebes after the beginning of the Twelfth Dynasty may be to a great extent ascribed to the influence and power of this 'hidden' god whose light soon blazed forth from beneath the bushel. There was, of course, much more to the greatness

86

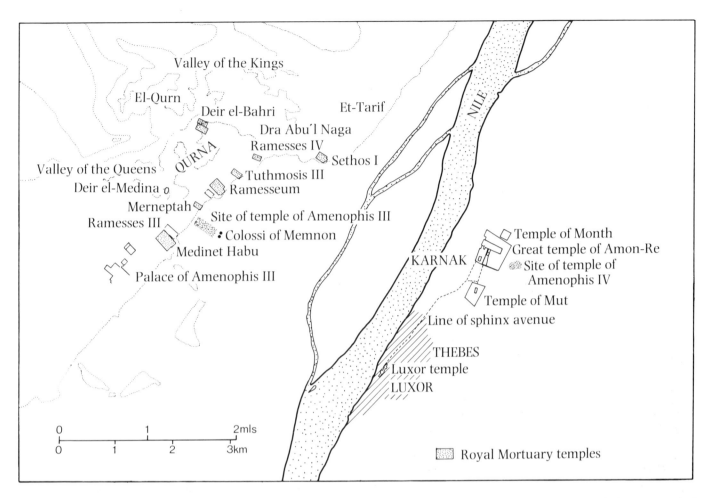

Valley of the Kings

El-Qurn

Deir el-Bahri                    Et-Tarif

                    Dra Abu'l Naga
                    Ramesses IV

QURNA                               Sethos I

Valley of the Queens            Tuthmosis III

Deir el-Medina o

            Ramesseum

Merneptah

Ramesses III        Site of temple of Amenophis III

            Colossi of Memnon

        Medinet Habu

Palace of Amenophis III

NILE

                    Temple of Month
                    Great temple of Amon-Re
KARNAK              Site of temple of
                    Amenophis IV

                    Temple of Mut

            Line of sphinx avenue

            THEBES

            Luxor temple
            LUXOR

0        1              2mls
0    1       2       3km

▦ Royal Mortuary temples

Thebes and the Theban
necropolis.

**86** *(opposite)* Silver figure, with
gold embellishments, of Amon-
Re, great god of Thebes.

**87** *(overleaf)* The colonnade of
Horemheb in the Temple of
Luxor. This area was filled with
buildings up to the mid-
nineteenth century. On the
right, the minaret of the
mosque of Abu'l Haggag.

of Thebes than Amun alone, but even in political terms the continued dominance of
Thebes among Egyptian cities owed much to the presence of the great sanctuaries of the
god and of his associated deities. They were in effect the local industrial giants, the mega-
corporations, which generated a mass of business subsidiary to the practice of the cults
and a huge army of officials and working people. And then there was the equally huge
necropolis enterprise on the west bank, which will be the subject of the next chapter. A
vast, interlocking nexus of activities sustained the region for many centuries. Decline
was slow, again lasting for many centuries; politics were largely responsible; collapse
was sudden and almost total.

When Thebes lapsed into its long twilight age which lasted up to the early nineteenth
century, the strange neglect had almost a beneficial effect on the preservation of its great
monuments. They had been much damaged in the years of collapse and destruction, but
for many subsequent centuries they passed almost unnoticed by the local inhabitants,
Copts and Moslems, who found their meaningless hieratic hulks convenient places for
villages. And so it may still seem to be to some extent today, although things are greatly
improved since the early nineteenth century when Henry Salt acquired a fine house in
the middle of the Luxor temple.

Our consideration of eastern Thebes, the modern town of Luxor, may start either at the
northern end, where the huge extent of the Karnak complex encapsulates the essence of

divine, imperial Egypt, or at the south where the graceful Luxor temple invariably refreshes the spirit. There is much to be said for starting at the southern end, for here has been the focus of Luxor life ever since visitors began to invade the ancient sites of Egypt in the early nineteenth century. It is also generally thought that the actual settlement of Wese lay in the area between the Luxor temple and the main Karnak temple (a distance of about one and a half miles from each other), with its centre roughly in what is now the commercial and bazaar district of Luxor – 'down-town Luxor', as I have heard it called by disorientated tourists. Throughout Egypt, modern towns and villages stand on top of ancient towns and villages. The processes of urban decay and rebuilding follow what could be described almost as an organic cycle, the old giving way to the new, with at the same time the raising of the new that little bit higher, to escape the depredations of the annual flood. In consequence the modern town of Luxor rides relatively high on the remains of ancient Luxor, and very little of the houses, great and small, and of the industrial establishments which would have made the place so lively and bustling in antiquity, has been excavated. Most of what has been cleared away in modern times to disburden the great temples and to open up the beginning of the processional way from Luxor to Karnak, has been unceremoniously ditched into the Nile, or used to bank up the corniche river-front and gardens which now extend along the Nile for about two miles from south to north.

For the first half of the nineteenth century the Karnak temple was the principal attraction for visitors on the east bank. The noble pylons of the Luxor temple were visible, protruding from great mounds of debris, along with the upper parts of colossal statues of Ramesses II, and, after 1831, one obelisk; its pair had in that year been removed, with official approval, by the French and now stands in the centre of the Place de la Concorde in Paris. It is said that among the negotiations which preceded the lowering and removal of this obelisk, one of the most difficult and protracted was the determination of compensation to be paid to the owners of thirty houses or more clustered around the granite shaft and impeding the path to the river's edge. This crowded precinct before the pylons gives only a small indication of the clutter and squalor that were to be found in the temple itself.

Today's visitor descends about twenty feet below the level of the corniche-road to reach the pavement in front of the great pylons. Scarcely more than one hundred years ago fifty feet of debris, mostly decayed houses, encumbered the temple, making it inaccessible to visitors. Here, among the colonnades and massive sculptures, were great houses and shrines, including a mansion belonging to Mustafa Agha Ayat, for many years the British Consular Agent in Luxor (acting also in the same capacity for Belgium and Russia), who entertained selected visitors lavishly and made a fortune from the illicit sale of antiquities. Among his neighbours for seven years in the 1860s was Lucie Duff Gordon, wife of Sir Alexander Duff Gordon, who abandoned the life of literary society in London and came to Egypt in search of a climate beneficial to her consumptive condition. She established herself high among the columns of the Luxor temple in the house once occupied by Henry Salt and which in the meanwhile had been temporary home for several well-known pioneer Egyptologists, including the great Champollion and the distinguished Italian Ippolito Rosellini. It had come to be known as the *Maison de France*. 'I have such a big rambling house all over the top of the temple of Khem (the old

88 The Reverend Greville
Chester, a great and responsible
nineteenth-century collector, in
the court of Amenophis III in
the temple of Luxor. In the
background is the colonnade of
King Horemheb.

designation of Min, the fertility-form of Amon-Re). How I wish I had you and the chicks
to fill it!', wrote Lady Duff Gordon to her husband soon after she had taken up
occupation. 'The view all round my house is magnificent on every side, over the Nile in
front facing north-west, and over a splendid range of green and distant orange buff hills
to the south-east, where I have a spacious covered terrace. It is rough and dusty to the
extreme, but will be very pleasant.' Nothing could seem to be more natural than to live
on a temple.

It is unlikely that attitudes changed much until the Antiquities Service in Egypt, newly
formed in 1858, began the systematic clearance – one could not call the work excavation
– of the great temples in Upper Egypt. Under its first director, Auguste Mariette, and his
successor, Gaston Maspero, hidden marvels of ancient architecture were revealed, not
least in the temple of Luxor. Even so, clearance was painfully slow; much remained to be
done up to and after the Second World War, and even now the charming, very ancient
and much revered mosque of Abu'l Haggag remains, occupying part of the temple's first
court. Its presence, compromising – as it seems – the integrity of a much earlier building,
tends to disturb visitors, who cannot understand why 'the authorities' are quite unable,
indeed, unwilling, to effect its removal. In fact, between the wars a real attempt was
made to induce its faithful to abandon the old mosque for a new place of worship not one
hundred yards away. But Moslem piety was not to be tempted; too many deep-rooted
traditions, cemented by real devotion, personally to the local saint Abu'l Haggag and
territorially to his shrine, rendered the expectation of success wholly nugatory. And so it
remains, its rear wall projecting incongruously into the temple court, reminding us of
that organic growth of towns and of buildings and demonstrating most graphically how
deep in rubble the temple already was when the foundations of the mosque were laid.

In a sense the continuous occupation of the temple by a large settlement from the time
of late antiquity onwards succeeded in protecting much of the building from grievous
damage. In consequence, since its clearance there is much more to wonder at, not least
the deep cut graffiti of foreign visitors in the early nineteenth century at the highest levels
of the columns, which once were easily accessible from the mounds of debris. Amelia B.
Edwards lamented the impossibility of seeing the greater part of the temple when she
visited it in 1874, and later, commending the clearance by the Antiquities Service, she
recalled in one part 'a labyrinthine maze of mud structures numbering some thirty
dwellings', and eighty straw sheds besides yards, stables and pigeon towers', and in
another, 'sheepfolds, goat-yards, poultry-yards, donkey-sheds, clusters of mud huts,
refuse heaps, and piles of broken pottery'.

It is almost possible to regret the disappearance of such a picturesque, though squalid,
shambles. But it is surely better to be able to walk the whole length of the temple's axis
without hindrance; to admire the towering pylons, the lone remaining obelisk and
shattered colossi; to pass into the great court of Ramesses II, still dominated by many
huge sculptures of the great king; to stroll along the majestic colonnade of Horemheb,
which was started by Amenophis III and resumed by Tutankhamun; to enter and
wonder at the most delicate and elegant of courts built under Amenophis III; and to
explore the complex of rooms at the south end, including the massive shrine inscribed for
Alexander the Great and the room in which Amenophis III celebrated the divine nature
of his birth in a series of tableaux.

89 (overleaf) The sphinx avenue
leading to the temple of Luxor,
and, in the opposite direction,
to the temple of Karnak. These
sphinxes were erected in the
reign of King Nectanebo I in
about 370 BC.

87

88

Let us, however, remember why the Luxor temple stands where it is. The gods worshipped here were essentially the same as those found at Karnak: principally Amun, his divine wife, the vulture-goddess Mut, and their divine child, the falcon-headed moongod Khons. But there were subtle differences between the Amun of Karnak and the Amun of Luxor, the former being closely associated with the sun-god Re and the latter in particular with Min, the fertility god of Coptos. In both places Amun was commonly called Amon-Re. Luxor was in a sense a place of retreat; it was called 'the southern harem', and rooms to the south of the shrine have been identified as a kind of suite of private apartments for use by the divine family. It was appropriate that the celebration of the divine conception and birth of Amenophis III, mentioned above, should be memorialised near by.

Amun of Luxor made regular visits to Thebes of the west bank in a function connected with the ceremonies of the necropolis, and he was visited annually in the second month of the inundation season by Amun of Karnak, accompanied by Mut and Khons of Karnak. This was the great Opet (harem) festival, the greatest of Theban religious celebrations, which was often graced by royal attendance. The opening, and most dramatic, event in the festival was the journey by river from Karnak to Luxor, each deity in its own boat and accompanied by bands of priests, bevies of dancers, a spirited braying of trumpets and other instruments, and processions of armed and unarmed attendants. Many incidents in this great gala are shown on the walls of the colonnade of Horemheb, and anyone today who wants to taste something of the common enthusiasm and fervour attending the event should visit Luxor during the feast of Abu'l Haggag, when the saint's portable boat is taken from his mosque in the Luxor temple and conducted around the streets of the town. It is not a simple survival of a very ancient ceremony, but it incorporates a folk-memory of something great and significant in the past. It is difficult for the curious and observant visitor to avoid tripping over such memories wherever he goes in Egypt. Even the name Thebes may have its origin in Ta-ipet, an abbreviated form of 'southern harem'.

If Amun of Karnak found the river journey the most spectacular way to travel to Luxor, the most direct route, and probably the one most used throughout antiquity was by land along the processional way, the beginning and end of which can still be seen, marked by sphinx avenues. At the Luxor end a substantial length with very well-preserved sphinxes of the Thirtieth Dynasty has been excavated since the Second World War. After about 200 yards it disappears under modern Luxor, but its path can be guessed if not actually traced, travelling in a north-easterly direction until remains of human-headed sphinxes emerge again just before the main Karnak temple is reached. Here the line seems to be making for the tenth pylon of the temple, built by King Horemheb right in the south enclosure wall. But there is some confusion here, for an easily traced massive avenue of ram-headed sphinxes leads directly from the same pylon to the enclosure of the temple of Mut, a dependency of Karnak. Furthermore, another avenue, this time of rams (divine animals of Amon-Re), leads from the formal gateway before the entrance to the temple of Khons in Karnak, to join the sphinx-avenue from Luxor. It seems reasonable to conclude that several avenues led out southwards from the Karnak temple, ultimately to unite in the main avenue.

Before entering the main Karnak complex, let us step aside where the avenues seem to

90 Head of one of the many statues of the lioness goddess Sakhmet found in the temple of Mut at Karnak. This benign-looking deity had a fearsome reputation in Egyptian mythology.

89

91 Granite head and arm from
a colossal sculpture, probably of
King Amenophis III, in the
temple of Mut at Karnak.

92 Colossal granite torso lying
in the temple of Mut at Karnak.
It was excavated by Belzoni in
the early nineteenth century.
The head and arm are shown
in fig. 91.

divide, and glance at the remarkable temple of Mut – Mut, Lady of Asheru, consort of Amun. Asheru was the name of the kidney-shaped lake next to which the temple was built. Its hey-day was in the Eighteenth Dynasty, but it saw much addition and rebuilding in the Twenty-fifth Dynasty and later. Here was one of the most fruitful areas for antiquity-hunting in the early days of Egyptian exploration. Scholars with Napoleon's expedition unearthed some of the huge number of statues of the lioness-headed goddess Sakhmet which stood and sat around the open courts of the temple, and even more were dug out and removed by Giovanni Battista Belzoni, who did so much for Henry Salt (and for himself) on both sides of the Nile at Thebes. It has been a commonplace to deride Belzoni's methods as crude and piratical, but in fact, as a reading of his entertaining *Narrative* may show, he had real interest in what he was unearthing and great sensitivity towards the achievements of the ancient Egyptians. He comes close to deserving the title of first excavator in Egypt, although he occasionally displays weaknesses of technique which tend to modify his credibility.

In spite of the large number of Sakhmet statues which have over the last two centuries been removed from the Mut temple, many still remain, peering benevolently through the tall grass and over crumbling walls at the occasional visitor. Few still realise that this somewhat maiden-aunt-like goddess had a history of violence and ferocity in her dealings with mortal man. On entering the temple the visitor may also see, within the enclosure and a little to the east of the entrance, a fallen, headless granite colossus. It is almost certainly the torso which Belzoni uncovered with the help of Henry Beechey,

90

92

secretary to Henry Salt: 'On my return from Gournou (on the west bank), I had the pleasure to find the discovery had been made of a colossal head . . . It was of red granite, of beautiful workmanship, and uncommonly well preserved, except one ear, and part of the chin, which had been knocked off along with the beard.' Belzoni gives no indication of where he found this splendid piece, and until recently it was though that it came from the main Karnak temple. A piece of clever detective work has now married up, as they say, the head with the Mut temple torso, and also the great arm which provides young visitors to the British Museum with the opportunity to measure their own right arms against something truly monumental. Unfortunately the torso, kindly examined on all sides by most obliging excavators from The Brooklyn Museum, has failed to yield an inscription which would identify the king portrayed. So a long-standing debate can continue, based on slender and shifting evidence; is it Tuthmosis III, or Amenophis III, or Ramesses II? For the moment let us split the difference.

As far as one can judge from his very unspecific account, Belzoni also found in the Mut temple a rare statue of Sethos II of the Nineteenth Dynasty (c 1214–1204 BC). It shows the king seated on a throne and holding on his knees a small shrine surmounted by a ram's head; it is made of an unusual whitish quartzite, a very hard stone, here worked with consummate skill, and is almost perfect; even the nose, that so vulnerable organ, has survived. Belzoni, with some justification, held it to be a statue of Jupiter Ammon.

The temple of Mut was to witness another, very unusual, excavation towards the end of the nineteenth century. On to the scene came Miss Margaret Benson, daughter of Edward White Benson, the Archbishop of Canterbury, and a sister of the novelist E.F. Benson. A visit to Egypt in 1894 gave her the, for those days, extraordinary idea to excavate in the temple of Mut – just a little clearance and tidying up. Undaunted, she put in an application for permission to dig in 1895, and after a first refusal received much support from influential Egyptologists who, presumably, felt that with supervision, some good, and probably no harm, might come of the enterprise. Permission was granted to her and to her friend Janet Gourlay, and for three seasons they worked for a few weeks on a modest scale on the temple site. The outcome was far beyond expectation, for they came upon a number of deposits of discarded statuary which included a fine block figure of Senenmut, right-hand man of Queen Hatshepsut, a number of royal statues of the Eighteenth and Nineteenth Dynasties and a quite extraordinary bust now in the Cairo Museum; it is from a statue of Mentuemhat, mayor of Thebes at the end of the Twenty-fifth Dynasty and in the early years of the Twenty-sixth Dynasty. A very sensitive head, of the same period as Mentuemhat, is carved anachronistically in the style of the Fifth Dynasty, almost 2,000 years earlier. Such was the success of the first lady excavators in Egypt. Virtue and ability were surely rewarded.

To walk from the seemingly remote and utterly peaceful temple of Mut to the vast complex known as the temple of Karnak is to move from a dream of the past to a bedlam of the present – a crowded, bustling, noisy, archaeological department-store, containing something for everyone. It is a walk of a few hundred yards only, but it is a walk back to reality encapsulated in a group of buildings which spans 2,000 years. And yet even here, so huge is the sacred precinct, there are many corners where the bemused visitor may collect his thoughts and contemplate quietly what lies before him. But the first thing to be done at Karnak is to establish the lay-out of the buildings occupying the precinct, which is encircled by great mud-brick walls enclosing an area of almost 62 acres. The main temple of Amon-Re should be traversed along its west-east axis, a distance of a quarter of 103 a mile. Thought may be given to the number of other great religious buildings in the world which might be accommodated in its space, but such would be an idle exercise, for space is not all there is to great religious buildings. It is pointless to compare the great temple of Amon-Re with, for example, St Peter's in Rome or Notre-Dame in Paris, or Westminster Abbey. In the ordinary sense an Egyptian temple was not a place for common worship; it was a place for the celebration of the cult, an intimate ceremony which ideally was a private act of communion between king and god. At Karnak this act of communion was always something a little grander in scale than a simple act of offering to the god; but it never involved public worship as it is now understood.

The essential act took place in the sanctuary, and at Karnak sanctuaries came and went as successive developments took place over the centuries. The main shrine, the room in which the god's image was kept, was erected in its last form in the reign of Philip Arrhidaeus, the successor of Alexander the Great, who ruled Egypt for a few years after the great conqueror's death. It is a fine granite structure, carved with precise reliefs of ritualistic ceremonies and processions in which the boat of the god is paraded. Here was the find-spot of a graceful black granite boat – not one to be carried in procession – 94 containing a seated figure of Mutemuia, wife of King Tuthmosis IV, in the guise of the goddess Mut. It was found during work instituted by the Earl of Belmore during a visit to Egypt in 1817. Karnak was a great lucky-dip of a site in the early nineteenth century,

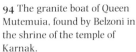

94 The granite boat of Queen Mutemuia, found by Belzoni in the shrine of the temple of Karnak.

95 Granite colossus of a king probably to be identified as Amenophis II, although carrying the names of Ramesses II and Merenptah.

96 Granite monument with high-relief figures of the king Tuthmosis III and the deities Month-Re and Hathor. The figures circle the monument holding hands.

and in spite of the need to obtain official permission to dig and remove objects, this simple formality was easily surmounted by those who understood the ways of persuasion. In consequence the whole sacred precinct was raided inconsequentially by distinguished visitors bent on acquiring a suitable souvenir or two of their journey.

Belzoni 'helped' a number of such visitors, at Karnak and elsewhere, in addition to conducting works on his own account and for his putative employer, Henry Salt. Among the sculptures which he states clearly to have come from Karnak, one which specially attracted him was what he calls 'an altar with the six divinities, in alto rilievo, which is the most finished work of any I have seen in Egypt'. It is a strange monument, the purpose of which has never satisfactorily been determined. The two short ends carry high relief figures of the goddess Hathor, and the two long sides figures of King Tuthmosis III and the god Month-Re, falcon-headed. King and deities circle the monument, holding hands in a timeless game of musical chairs. It is indeed finely carved, particularly the royal figures, both of which have sadly lost their heads. Belzoni claimed to have found it in a small temple in the north-east corner of the precinct, a part of the site which still remains to be excavated properly. A similar, but less well preserved, monument can now be seen in a room on the north side of the main temple axis just before the shrine is reached.

Karnak is still a site of undiscovered wonders and interests. Great works have cleared the main temple, the separate temple of Khons and much of the area around the sacred lake; they are now tackling the series of pylons and buildings leading from the mighty Hypostyle Hall to the southern gate and the avenue to the temple of Mut. An enterprising collaboration between Egyptian and French archaeologists and engineers is now engaged in the most comprehensive study of the precinct ever undertaken. The plums

96

97 The kiosk or 'way-station' of Sesostris I, a building reconstructed from blocks used to provide the filling for the second pylon of the Karnak temple.

99 A masterpiece of royal sculpture, portraying a mid-Eighteenth-Dynasty ruler, either Hatshepsut or Tuthmosis III. The stone is very hard green schist.

allowed to be sold to museums elsewhere, and there are now few important collections in Europe and North America which cannot show at least one statue from this remarkable cache, or cachette as it always called.

A much smaller, but very choice cache of sculpture was made known to Ernest Wallis Budge in about 1902, apparently outside the eastern wall of the Karnak precinct. Budge, at the time Keeper of Egyptian and Assyrian Antiquities in the British Museum, maintained good relations with many influential Egyptians in Luxor who were engaged in the antiquities trade. One of these gentlemen let Budge know that an underground chamber had been discovered, containing sculptures. In two rather contradictory accounts Budge describes the chamber as a kind of shrine, with a granite offering-table of King Amosis of the Eighteenth Dynasty in the middle. The whole was presided over by a fine limestone statue of Queen Hatshepsut, her 'court' containing four statues of important officials of the Eighteenth Dynasty, one of the Twenty-fifth Dynasty and one of the very end of the Dynastic period; there were also two inscriptions of workmen from the royal workmen's village in Western Thebes. Budge's fuller account is very circumstantial:

The chamber measured 8 feet by 6 feet, and was built of stones. In the centre on a dais was a massive granite altar bearing the name of Amosis I. At the west end of the chamber was a seated statue of Queen Hatshepsut made of a sort of soft-lead-stone with sparkles in it. At her right, on pedestals, were the two statues of Senenmut, and on her left were the two statues of Teti and Amenwahsu, also on pedestals. At the east end of the chamber stood the statue of Men-kheperresonb, and close by the statues of Pes-shu-per and Unnefer. By the side wall (on the north) were the two stelae. It seemed that the chamber was a sort of private funerary chapel, above which there had once stood a larger chamber.

Budge could scarcely be described as gullible, but there are so many peculiar features in his story that some kind of deception must be suspected. Were, for example, all the statues secretly retrieved from the great Karnak cachette and 'arranged' in this subterranean chamber to impress him? Who can now say? Budge claims to have shown the chamber to Georges Legrain, the French Egyptologist who was at the time clearing the cachette, and he reports no suggestion of suspicion. In due course the whole collection, less one, found its way with official permission to London. The statue of Hatshepsut is said to have crumbled to dust before it could be removed. Senenmut with little princess Neferure on his lap, enfolded in his cloak, is now one of the best-loved sculptures in the British Museum. Was he truly just the loyal servant of Queen Hatshepsut? The second Senenmut statue is altogether different, a formal block-statue of yellowish-brown quartzite, heavily inscribed with texts. It lacks the human and personal interest of the companion statue, and represents a much more traditional, if not conventional, way of presenting an important official. Its texts are designed to enable Senenmut to participate in the offerings to the gods in the great temple of Karnak; it is a true votive piece. Unhappily, the face of the subject has been deliberately defaced, an act of vengeance possibly perpetrated when Senenmut fell from grace. It is not impossible that he overreached himself in exploiting his special relationship with his queen, and paid the penalty of disgrace or even worse.

Of the other sculptures from Budge's problematical shrine, two in particular stand out as pieces of unusual merit. They are both carved from pinkish-purple quartzite, a very

100 Pes-shu-per shown as a scribe, a representation of an important Twenty-fifth-Dynasty official, in a form of sculpture dating to the Old Kingdom but with elements of Middle-Kingdom style.

101 Quartzite statuette of the high-priest of Month, Amenwahsu, found in Budge's Karnak 'shrine'. The great god of Karnak, depicted and invoked on the stela supported by Amenwahsu, is here called Amon-Re-Herakhty.

102 Senenmut nurses the princess Neferure, wrapped close in his cloak. A granite statue of the steward of Hatshepsut found in a strange 'shrine' at Karnak.

hard stone which takes a fine finish. Amenwahsu, a high-priest of Month, who lived probably towards the end of the Eighteenth Dynasty, kneels in an attitude of adoration, supporting in front of his body a stela, or formal inscription. The text is an invocation of the sun god, here named Re-Herakhty, and above is a charming, very crisply carved vignette of the god, with ram's head, standing in his sacred boat. He is 'Amon-Re-Herakhty, the great god, lord of heaven'. It has been suggested that in style and form this sculpture reproduces work of the mid-Eighteenth Dynasty in an archaising manner. The deriving of inspiration from the past was a common phenomenon of Egyptian sculpture, especially in later periods, and the process is even more admirably exemplified in the second quartzite piece. This shows Pes-shu-per, chamberlain of Amenardis, the extremely influential priestly princess who was virtual ruler of Thebes in the mid-Twenty-fifth Dynasty. Pes-shu-per is shown as a scribe, squatting on the ground and writing on an open papyrus laid on his kilt, which is tightly drawn over his knees. The statue-type dates back to the Old Kingdom, while his wig is of a characteristically Middle-Kingdom form. But the whole does not appear in any way a pastiche; it is made coherent and wholly satisfactory by the excellent workmanship and by a distinct lack of symmetry which would never have been found in a fine piece of earlier date. Intelligence and sympathy inform the features of this great man, who felt it no shame to be shown as a simple scribe.

After the long parade through the main temple of Amon-Re, and the inspection of the out-door 'museum' with the re-erected shrines of Sesostris I and Amenophis I, visitors are inclined to perambulate the Sacred Lake and walk towards the exit marked by the huge formal granite gate of Ptolemy III, Euergetes. This imposing portal stands in front of the entrance to the temple of Khons, the divine child in the Theban family of gods. The well-preserved temple has a coherence which is not to be found in the main temple of Amon-Re, even though, like the main temple, its construction and decoration continued over many centuries. It is essentially a building of the Twentieth Dynasty, and Khons was here worshipped in particular as Khons-Neferhotep, whose cult became very important in the late New Kingdom and subsequent periods. A remarkable late inscription purports to tell of an event that occurred in the reign of Ramesses II when Khons-Neferhotep arranged for his fellow deity Khons-the-Contriver to be sent to the distant land of Bakhtan to effect a miraculous cure. Such was the reputation of the Khons by the 'back-door' of Karnak. By assimilation he was also associated with Thoth, another moon-god, and as such commonly shown as a dog-headed ape, or baboon. Two small baboon figures once standing by the entrance to the Khons temple are now in London. As representations of Khons-Neferhotep and Khons-the-Contriver, they exercise their own particular magic in protecting many old Karnak friends and colleagues in an alien but sympathetic environment.

103 (overleaf) A general view over the main temple complex of Karnak, looking west from the Festival Hall of Tuthmosis III.

145

# CHAPTER SEVEN

# City of the Dead

## WESTERN THEBES

LIVE ON the east bank, die on the west. That, roughly, was the division of function at Thebes in antiquity. On the east bank, as we have just seen, were the great cult temples of Karnak and Luxor, and also the ancient city which was for so many centuries one of the most important centres of administrative power in Egypt, and the base of the Upper-Egyptian vizier. Paradoxically, however, if we want to know about life in Thebes during the great days of the Eighteenth and Nineteenth Dynasties, then we must turn to the west bank. For most of the evidence of ancient daily living can be derived from the eloquent scenes in the tombs of private personages, the great, influential, civil and religious officials, the small army of lesser dignitaries, and even some of the artist-craftsmen who helped to make and decorate the royal tombs. And from these same tombs come most of the well-preserved examples of ancient Egyptian furniture and other household equipment which add so much interest to the older collections of antiquities in the museums of Cairo, of Europe, and of the USA.

The Egyptian belief in the continuation of life after death, and the concomitant idea that proper provision should be made so that this posthumous extension could be properly enjoyed, resulted in the remarkable stocking of tombs with complete domestic equipments, varied only according to the status of the individual tomb's occupier. In many parts of Egypt unsatisfactory conditions have prevented the survival of such equipments, even when they have escaped the depredations of the tomb robber in antiquity, and of the antiquities hunter in modern times. Damp and the ravages of termites have caused most of the damage, and only during the present century have the techniques of archaeologists been successful, or partially so, in saving sadly decayed objects which in the nineteenth century would have certainly been utterly destroyed on discovery. In the Theban necropolis, however, conditions were peculiarly favourable for the preservation of objects, made of organic materials – wood, linen, papyrus, leather, reeds, even feathers. But to get to the material before it was discovered by the inhabitants of the villages integrated within the complicated geography of the tombs, was from the first a race in which all the odds were on the locals.

Tomb-robbery was a highly developed profession in ancient Egypt, and it seems likely that few rich burials survived comprehensive clearance within a relatively short period after the dead tomb-owner took up residence in his 'house of eternity'. Texts on papyri from the late Twentieth and Twenty-first Dynasties, containing the statements of apprehended tomb-robbers, make it quite clear that certain groups of artisans in ancient Thebes were well equipped to effect break-ins to royal and private tombs. One group of thieves was examined by a tribunal of very high officials, including the vizier, on day 14 of the third month in the season of inundation in the 16th year of King Ramesses IX

**104** One of a pair of fine bronze situlae acquired by Belzoni in the Theban necropolis. Pediamun-neb-nesut-tawy, a high priestly official of Thirtieth Dynasty date, adores Osiris.

(*c.* 1131–1112 BC). One of the thieves was Amenpanufer, a quarryman attached to the temple of Amun. His evidence, in part, runs as follows:

I went to the tombs of the west of Thebes together with the thieves who were with me (previously) at the tombs of the west of Thebes. We brought away the silver and the gold which we had found in the tombs and the offering vessel which we had found there, taking in our hands my bronze chisels and opening the coffin chests with the bronze chisels which we had in hand. And we brought away the inner coffins which were gilded, broke them up, and set fire to them by night in the tombs. And we gathered up the gold and silver which we found on them and took it (the gold and silver) and divided it for ourselves.

The brazen manner in which this evidence is given almost suggests pride on the part of the thief in his achievement. Similar statements preserved in other documents from the same archive display equal daring and an apparent equal willingness to 'tell all', as some of the malefactors proclaim. Some, under interrogation, even describe how they visited the tombs to rob 'as was our habit'. Here was an illicit activity which was not casual, but well organised – part of the ancient black economy of the Theban district. No doubt the depositions of the thieves, extracted usually with some painful persuasion, as is made quite clear, were to some extent edited, even as modern police statements may be helpfully translated into the parlance (or jargon) thought to be acceptable to the courts. Nevertheless, the quarryman Amenpanufer and his partners in crime emerge from these texts as real people, such as we never meet in the great metropolis on the east bank.

It is certainly true to say that this close acquaintance with Thebans of no special status is quite exceptional for the ancient Egyptian world, and it is multiplied many times over for the workmen and their families who lived in the village which had been founded by King Tuthmosis I (*c.* 1504–1492 BC) to accommodate the artists and craftsmen engaged on the cutting and decorating of royal tombs in the Valley of the Kings. These workmen were mostly literate, and they made prodigious use of limestone flakes to write every kind of small document, including accounts of squabbles, of legal actions, of commercial transactions, from which their individualities are readily appreciated. They are known by name, their families are known, their genealogies can often be traced for many generations. This close-knit community may serve as a microcosm of Egyptian society at a modest level, and we shall come back to it from time to time when our feet need to return to firm and human ground after visiting the extraordinary manifestations of the ambit of death which outstandingly characterise the Theban necropolis.

For the present, however, let us return to Amenpanufer and to his distant descendants, the inhabitants of early nineteenth century western Thebes, especially those of the village of Qurna, who took up again with enthusiasm the ancient profession of tomb-robbery which had lain dormant for very many centuries. Living in many cases actually in the ancient tomb-chapels, they were well acquainted with the nature of these

106

105

subterranean monuments, had little fear of any local ghosts (although they would be terrified to wander on the high desert by night), and were quick to appreciate the value of tomb equipment which in the past they had been content to burn. Old furniture and painted coffins fed their cooking fires; rolls of papyri gave off a pleasant fragrance when burnt, rather like joss-sticks. But now an old chair or a coffin would fetch good money, and even papyrus might be better sold than burned.

When travellers began visiting the Theban area after the end of Napoleon's Egyptian adventure, the trade in antiquities developed overnight. Everyone wanted a souvenir of his visit, and there was no shortage of suitably sized objects to satisfy the demand. Unfortunately, no care was applied in the acquisition of antiquities and probably more was destroyed in the process of recovery than was retrieved intact. To gain the trust of the tomb-dwellers was a privilege rarely enjoyed by Europeans, but Belzoni, who spent long periods of time living in western Thebes, was occasionally allowed to enter some of the secret regions under close supervision:

Of some of their tombs many persons could not withstand the suffocating air, which often causes fainting. A vast quantity of dust rises, so fine that it enters into the throat and nostrils, and chokes the nose and mouth to such a degree that it requires great power of lungs to resist it and the strong effluvia of the mummies.

Nevertheless, by being on the spot, and by securing a kind of intimate acquaintance with the active tomb-robbers, Belzoni was able to acquire a wide range of interesting material which passed to his patron Henry Salt and, in due course to the British Museum.

Not least of the problems to be overcome in dealing with the inhabitants of Qurna was the obsessive secrecy in which all transactions were conducted. Each discovery was reserved to be exploited by the individual discoverer and, possibly, his family; so sources had to be protected. Belzoni found himself on more than one occasion on the brink of being drawn into local feuds. He tells of one man who tried to engage in a little private enterprise without the knowledge of his associates:

... my guide told me by the way, that he had some papyri to sell, which he had himself found ... and it was agreed that I was to repair to his house alone to see them. However I took Mr. Beechey

105 (above left) The hillside of Qurna, site of fine decorated private tombs of the New Kingdom and home in the nineteenth century of the Egyptologist Sir J. Gardner Wilkinson.

106 (above right) The workmen's village at Deir el-Medina, an exclusive, but enclosed, settlement for the skilled craftsmen who worked on the royal tombs.

107 (opposite) Vignette from the Book of the Dead of Hunefer, a royal scribe. Hunefer's mummy, about to be placed in his tomb, receives the last rites which will enable the deceased to practise his bodily functions after death.

151

with me, and we had great difficulty to prevent those by whom we were observed from following us . . . When Mr. Beechey, myself, and the interpreter, entered his cave, his wife walked out to watch if any one approached . . . He made us sit down on a straw mat, which is a luxurious thing in Gournou [Qurna], and after a little ceremony, put into my hands a brazen vessel . . . It was covered with engraved hieroglyphics very finely executed . . . We were examining it with astonishment, when the old man took it from our hands, and presented us with another exactly similar to it.

Belzoni soon concluded a bargain, but it was several days before the owner was able to deliver the vessels because, he claimed, he was under surveillance. In the end it turned out that the whole business of secrecy was a charade and that the owner, acting for his syndicate, had secured beyond his price a fine red cap for himself. Belzoni had, however, secured, as he suspected, two of the finest bronze ritual vessels to have survived from antiquity.

In a sense, Belzoni's activities in the private tombs of Qurna formed a side-line to his principal operations in western Thebes. But before these are considered, some time may be devoted to the man who, more than anyone else, breathed life into the representations in the tombs, expounding in his *Manners and Customs of the Ancient Egyptians* what he summarised as 'their private life, government, laws, arts, manufactures, religions, and early history; derived from a comparison of the paintings, sculptures, and monuments still existing . . .' John Gardner Wilkinson came to Egypt in 1821, inspired by Sir William Gell, an antiquarian and friend of the physicist (and early partial decipherer of the hieroglyphic script) Thomas Young, to take up the study of ancient Egypt. Wilkinson remained for twelve years, building a house right in the middle of Qurna. Indefatigably he worked, copying scenes in the tombs, studying the detail of the representations, conducting modest excavations, and noting the many objects found by his Egyptian neighbours and those acquired by early collectors like Henry Salt. His notebooks and portfolios became the repository of a vast assemblage of information, including very accurate copies of scenes and texts. He was very much one of the founding fathers of Egyptology, and the very first to exploit in a comprehensive way the wealth of material which suddenly became available to scholars.

His percipience and humour render his great work a constant delight, and even now it is worth reading, and not simply as an antiquarian curiosity. He describes a banquet scene:

A party assembled at the house of a friend are regaled with the sound of music, and the customary introduction of refreshments; and no attention which the host could show his visitors appears to be neglected on the occasion. The wine has circulated freely, and as they are indulging in amusing converse, a young man, perhaps from inadvertence, perhaps from the effects of weight against a column in the centre of the apartment, throws it down upon the assembled guests; who are seen, with uplifted hands, endeavouring to protect themselves, and escape from its fall.

Unusually, no illustration accompanies this account, for as Wilkinson disarmingly notes: 'I regret exceedingly having mislaid the copy I made of this amusing subject.' In the case of a very fine model granary formerly in Salt's collection, he compares the structure with what could still be observed in villages in nineteenth-century Egypt. He further remarks:

108 Model granary. The overseer or owner looks down on the court which houses the grain bins; a woman grinds barley.

In the court a woman was represented making bread, as is sometimes done at the present day in Egypt, in the open air; and the storerooms were not only full of grain when the model was found, but would have still preserved their contents uninjured had they escaped the notice of a rat in the lazaretto of Leghorn, which in one night destroyed what ages had respected.

So it may be seen today, with the lady bread maker busily at work grinding the grain that 108 no longer survives.

To compare the copies of tomb scenes made by Wilkinson and others in the early nineteenth century with what remains to be seen today is to appreciate not only the value of the early copies, but also the tragic depredations wrought in the tombs by vandalism, mindless theft and sheer carelessness. It is even possible to forgive the removal from certain tombs of substantial fragments which have at least survived without further damage in the protected environments of museums. A group of such fragments was taken to London in the 1820s. The circumstances of their removal from the Theban necropolis are undocumented; the site of the actual tomb-chapel is unknown; even the name of the tomb-owner is uncertain; but the quality and interest of the paintings are outstanding. It is most probable that Henry Salt was responsible for their shipment to London, and he may also have arranged for their removal; but it may be surmised that if he were the agent of removal, he countenanced the action because of the threat of destruction. It seems not to have been his practice wilfully to dismantle standing monuments, although he certainly arranged for the removal of detached reliefs and individual sculptures.

Nebamun, an agricultural official, is thought to have been the owner of this tomb – part of a name which could thus be restored is preserved on one fragment – and it is generally accepted that he exercised his important, but not very high, office in the reign of Amenophis III. But whatever his position in the hierarchy of Theban bureaucracy, he succeeded in obtaining the services of a remarkable artist (or even of two artists) to carry out the decorative scheme in his tomb-chapel. The finest surviving fragment, in which Nebamun is shown hunting birds in a marshy thicket, has already been briefly described 10 in the discussion of the Delta as a place of recreation. Here we may note especially the rich depiction of natural detail; birds, fish, butterflies, the stylised, yet wholly convincing, papyrus thicket, and above all the tabby cat who retrieves for his master. Egyptian artists are specially renowned for their lifelike representations of animals and birds, and the bronze cats produced in the late Dynastic Period are rightly admired for their dignity of 11 form and splendid modelling; but no cat is more vibrant with life, more lithe in posture, more convincingly feral, in short, more cat-like, than Nebamun's assistant. And the painting of its fur is quite exceptional.

Indeed his ability to render texture and shading by a masterly control of a limited range of colours and very primitive brushes sets this artist well apart from most of his contemporaries. In other fragments, in which scenes of cattle- and geese-counting are shown, the same techniques are employed to represent and differentiate large numbers of similar creatures in ways which successfully avoid the somewhat formal and wooden appearance of many contemporary, comparable scenes.

While the bird-hunting scene is by far the easiest to appreciate as a painting in terms of modern appreciation – it has coherence, a strong visual focus of interest and a finely balanced and precisely placed pattern of secondary detail – it should not be forgotten that

109 Part of the banqueting
scene from the tomb of
Nebamun: music is played and
dancing girls gyrate.

its present appearance is the result of fortuitous survival. It originally formed part of a
much larger, double scene in which Nebamun was also shown spearing fish. The chance
which allows us to appreciate what now can be seen as a wholly satisfactory graphic
composition should be measured, and in a sense corrected, by looking at other fragments
from the same tomb in which the essentially linear mode of composition, regularly
employed by the Egyptians, can be seen. Two large parts of an extensive banqueting
scene display this compositional phenomenon admirably. Guests at this feast, which is
both funerary and celebratory, sit in pairs, ranged in line left to right. From the hand of a
conventional painter such arrangements tend to be repetitive and dull, even if individual
figures are executed with skilled and stylish draughtsmanship. Nebamun's painter,

however, has introduced variety and vitality by disposing the couples individually and collectively in changing postures, by varying detail, by modifying gestures. And in the representation of the group of musicians and dancers, he has excelled himself; the dancing girls weave and bend in a way that completely negates the commonly held view that Egyptian art is stiff and formal; two of the musicians are shown full-face and with bodies also represented frontally. The latter group is sensationally innovative, even if it is difficult to decide whether the innovation is a complete success.

The exploitation of western Thebes as a place of burial was the inevitable result of the political developments of the early Middle Kingdom which brought to national power the local ruling house. The west for the Egyptians was the place of the setting sun, the nearest region they could come to identifying as the realm of the justified dead. At Thebes the possibilities for development were remarkably promising – a wide, cultivated plain leading to foothills, ideally shaped for the placing of innumerable rock-cut tombs,

110 Gilded cartonnage mummy mask of a princess, probably from a burial of the late Middle Kingdom at Thebes, in the region named Dra Abu'l Naga.

found the cache in the 1860s or early 1870s. Some items from this extraordinary Aladdin's Cave of mortuary remains filtered out into the antiquities market and some very fine papyri in due course found their way to European museums and notably to London and the British Museum: in 1903 the *Book of the Dead* of Queen Nodjmet, presented by King Edward VII, who had been given it on his visit to Egypt in 1876; in 1910, the *Book of the Dead* of the princess Nesitanebtashru, remarkable for its finely drawn ink vignettes, and for being the longest known text of this religious compilation (over 150 feet); in 1960, a further roll of the same text, written for the High-priest of Amun, Pinudjem. This last, acquired in 1874 by Sir Archibald Campbell in Luxor, was one of the items which alerted Maspero, head of the Egyptian Antiquities Service, to the fact that an important cache of antiquities had been discovered in the Theban area and was being clandestinely exploited.

112 Two wooden 'guardian' royal figures found by Belzoni in tombs in the Valley of the Kings. In the middle, the inner gilded wooden coffin of the lady Henutmehit.

When the location of the cache was finally disclosed to the authorities – the consequence of a dispute within the family of robbers – the bodies of twelve of Egypt's kings were discovered, including some of the very greatest, Amenophis I, Tuthmosis III, Sethos I, Ramesses II and Ramesses III. It is said that as the boats carrying these regal

113 An episode from the
Satirical Papyrus in which
animals perform human
activities: a lion and an
antelope play *senet*, an Egyptian
board-game.

remains sailed north from Luxor, the women of the villages of Western Thebes ran along the river-bank, throwing dust on their heads and ululating, as if they followed the funeral cortège of some great person recently dead. Such, they said, was the depth of their concern – a spontaneous demonstration of traditional grief. The cynic might comment that what they lamented was the loss of a fortune, denied to the rich trade in *antikas*. The cup had been dashed from the thirsty lips.

Since antiquity many of the royal tombs in the Valley remained open, accessible to visitors and to the indefatigable scribblers of graffiti. But the best tomb, in terms of mural decoration, although robbed in ancient times, remained to be discovered and opened in the early nineteenth century by Belzoni. He was the first to investigate the Valley of the Kings and it was his privilege to be the first in modern times to enter the tomb of Sethos I of the Nineteenth Dynasty, the reliefs and paintings in which are of the very highest quality. It is greatly to Belzoni's credit that his first expressions of admiration were lavished on the tomb and its decoration – by this appreciation he distinguished himself as being no common antiquities-hunter – but he reserved his greatest praise for the alabaster sarcophagus of the king, a remarkable coffer, exquisitely and intricately carved with a veritable corpus of royal funerary texts. It can now be seen in the Sir John Soane Museum in Lincoln's Inn Fields in London, where it was carried in triumph by Soane after the Trustees of the British Museum had refused to buy it from Henry Salt at what he regarded as a bargain price of £2,000.

In Belzoni's day the Valley of the Kings was still a remote place, the valley floor encumbered with mounds of rubble. Inhabited by ghosts and the memories of glorious and ancient ceremonies, it held promise of great discoveries. Belzoni's pioneer operations in opening up a number of tombs were followed much later in the nineteenth century and into the twentieth by excavators of the Antiquities Service and other licensed investigators. Further tombs were found, some of which still held remarkable objects; that of Amenophis II with a further cache of royal mummies; that of Iuyia and Tjuiu, the parents of Tiye, wife of Amenophis III, with all its funeral furniture; and, above and

112

159

beyond all expectation, the virtually intact tomb of Tutankhamun. Nothing of consequence has been found since that last great discovery in 1922, and the Valley today retains little of its former mystery. Now tourist buses pound a metalled road along a way formerly winding and rough but now unkinked and lacking in magic. A quick glance catches sight of Howard Carter's house on an isolated knob of rock, and one is deposited in an ever-increasing bus park, surrounded by souvenir-sellers, and crowds of tourists, who are no better and no worse than oneself.

Some feeling for the Valley's old and special atmosphere can be gained by a visit to the relatively remote tomb of Tuthmosis III, high up in the sheer rock-wall at the deepest 115 corner of the sacred enclave. Here the cliffs rise close and threatening, and the relative solitude allows the imagination to expand. It is also good to escape from the Valley by the hill path which leads from beyond the entrance to the tomb of Sethos I. From the half-way point, high above the Valley, with the pyramidal form of the peak known as El-Qurn (the horn) rising in front, a fine conspectus can be gained of the main Valley, of its side 'tributaries', of the winding way to the cultivation and from thence to the Nile. From here an appreciation can be obtained of the reasons which led the royal advisers in the early Eighteenth Dynasty to choose this seemingly remote spot for royal entombments. How sad that their expectations of security were so regularly frustrated by the ingenuity and skills of the Theban tomb-robbers, aided without a doubt by accomplices among the necropolis guard!

From the intermediate plateau above the Valley of the Kings the way may be taken 106 either to the workmen's village at Deir el-Medina or round the lip of the great amphitheatre of Deir el-Bahri and by a steep downward path to Hatshepsut's temple which has made it the most striking of Theban sites. First, a quick visit to the workmen. More has been learned about the life of ordinary Egyptians from what has survived at Deir el-Medina than from the yield of any other site in Egypt. During the nineteenth century the village and its periphery was a happy hunting ground for antiquities collectors, and most museums contain large numbers of the small votive inscriptions set up by the workmen and their families. Regular excavations then uncovered the whole village, preserved remarkably well because the houses were stone-built and not of unbaked mud-brick as was regular elsewhere. From time to time large numbers of inscribed limestone flakes and pot-sherds, and even papyri, were discovered. The workmen were, as we have already mentioned, mostly literate and they exercised their ability to write with lavish abundance. In consequence, the inhabitants of this specialist community are unusually well known. They recorded their business transactions, their quarrels, their favourite literature; they practised their graphic skills, trying out conventional scenes, caricaturing their friends and the great whom they served, 113 parodying the activities of men in the guise of animals. The so-called Satirical Papyrus shows typical tomb scenes, except that it is a lion who plays *senet* (a board-game) with an antelope; it is a fox who herds cattle, playing double pipes as he goes; it is a cat who drives geese to the census. Anyone who spends some time in the study of Egypt will appreciate the humanity of the ancient inhabitants of the Nile Valley; time spent with the voluminous documentation of Deir el-Medina proves beyond a doubt that this humanity is of a kind and quality scarcely distinguishable from that of men and women today.

The second path from the rocky saddle above the Valley of the Kings leads eventually,

**114** Pillar with a colossal figure of King Amenophis I in the form of Osiris: part of an avenue leading to a small temple of that king at Deir el-Bahri.

as we have said, to the amphitheatre of Deir el-Bahri. As the path skirts the cliff, a fine view for those who can endure heights can be had almost vertically down to the buildings below: the terraced originality of Hatshepsut's funerary temple, the much ruined podium of Nebhepetre Mentuhotpe's tomb, and the even more ruined temple platform which once held a temple of Tuthmosis III, discovered since the Second World War by Polish archaeologists who have been responsible also for the latest reconstructions in Hatshepsut's temple. The proper way to view this famous monument is from ground level, advancing towards it from the east, following roughly the line of the causeway which in antiquity formed the ceremonial approach to the temple. Generally speaking, the ancient Egyptians did not evidently consider the setting of a great building before proceeding with its construction. It could be argued that the Step Pyramid at Saqqara and the Great Pyramid at Giza were consciously placed on their desert plateau sites so as to be seen clearly from the cultivated valley of the Nile, and in a sense dominate the sky-line. But no other Egyptian building is so intimately integrated into its setting as Hatshepsut's temple. With the stunning backdrop of the pinkish limestone cliffs of Deir el-Bahri towering over the site, the successive terraces of the temple rise gradually and most effectively to provide a series of horizontally precise colonnades to offset the vertical lines of the natural setting.

Although the queen's temple now completes the drama of this theatrical scene, her architects cannot be credited wholly with the choice of such an original site. As we have mentioned, an equally original structure formed the tomb complex of King Nebhepetre, and there is much archaeological evidence to suggest that Deir el-Bahri was a place favoured by kings of the Twelfth Dynasty and of the early Eighteenth Dynasty. Excavations by the Egypt Exploration Fund in the early twentieth century yielded discoveries of remarkable sculptures, including a dramatic head of Nebhepetre, wearing the white crown of Upper Egypt, a colossal figure of Amenophis I in the form of Osiris, and a series of splendid black granite life-size statues of Sesostris III of the Twelfth Dynasty now in Cairo and London. Of this last group, all four of which are striking examples of the fine Middle-Kingdom portraiture, one in particular stands out as being exceptional, and can truly justify the highest claim of masterpiece. The characteristic lineaments of this king's features may be distinguished in this sculpture; but here they are modelled with a sensitive strength and extraordinary subtlety; it may not be a true likeness, but it is a stunningly interpretive portrait of responsible kingship. There is nothing conventional here.

Hatshepsut's mortuary temple is additionally so sited as to be, in a sense, back to back with the Valley of the Kings. It was as close to the Valley as could be managed, allowing for the intervening rocky hill over which led the path to Deir el-Bahri. For most royal burials, however, the corresponding funerary temples were built on the very edge of the desert foothills, skirting the line of the cultivation; at the northern end lies the temple of Sethos I, and at the south, at Medinet Habu, that of Ramesses III; the former again displays the remarkable quality of relief carving so characteristic of that king; the latter is the best preserved of all and is of special interest in having accommodated within its precinct the necropolis administration during the later New Kingdom.

Of the intermediate temples along this line, the best known and most visited is the Ramesseum, the vast mortuary chapel of Ramesses II. But perhaps even more distinctive

117

114

116

**115** *(left)* The Valley of the Kings, with the entrance to the Tomb of Tutankhamun; the dominating peak is El-Qurn.

**116** *(above)* A study in responsible kingship: one of the granite statues of Sesostris III from Deir el-Bahri.

**117** *(right)* Amon-Re, in the temple of Hatshepsut at Deir el-Bahri, sits in receipt of a wide range of offerings.

immensely rich area, the whole can be peopled with a vast population of priests, bureaucrats, artists, craftsmen, workmen and simple villagers, with their families. Western Thebes in antiquity was the city of the dead, the necropolis *par excellence*. It was also a bustling and vibrant community, most of the members of which lived by the commerce of death and burial. It was all in a day's work; and no doubt the overwhelming pall of doom and the afterlife which is so strongly sensed by today's visitor made little impression on the ancient inhabitants of the necropolis. They were scarcely tourists in their own back-yard, and probably felt, if anything, a kind of homely communion with their deceased neighbours, just like the modern Cairenes who live among the graves in the City of the Dead. But the abiding natural image then as now is the range of the Theban hills to the west, dominated by El-Qurn, blushing pink in the morning sun, and glowing red as the chocolate-box sun descends in the west at dusk – the god Re returning to his night-time boat to travel the path so dramatically laid out in the great descending corridors of the royal tombs of the Valley of the Kings. Egypt is a land of striking continuity.

**119** Two seated granite colossal statues of King Amenophis III, from the royal mortuary temple in Western Thebes.

# The Head of the South

## SOUTHERN UPPER EGYPT

I was one whom my lord loved, and praised every day. I passed a considerable period of years under the majesty of my lord, the Horus Wahankh, King of Upper and Lower Egypt, son of Re, Inyotef, while this land was under his control, southwards to Abu and ending at Tjeni in the Thinite nome.

These words form part of what is generously called the autobiographical text of Tjetji, a   120
high Theban official who served as treasurer to the Kings Inyotef II and III of the early Eleventh Dynasty (c. 2118–2069 BC). It is inscribed on a splendid limestone monument – perhaps the finest surviving private record of the period – which most probably came from the west Theban district of Dra Abu'l Naga, where the early Eleventh-Dynasty royal tombs were located. Now Tjetji had his inscription carved towards the end of the turbulent, obscure time known as the First Intermediate Period, when no universal royal power was exercised throughout the land of Egypt. It is clear that at first, after the disintegration of central control from Memphis at the end of the Sixth Dynasty, the provincial notables, the nomarchs who administered the departments or nomes of Egypt, were able to exercise power locally for some time, their success depending very much on the relationships they were able to build up with their neighbouring notables. In northern Upper Egypt, a coalition based on the nome of Heracleopolis established a very considerable power base, as we have already observed in Chapter 3.

In southern Upper Egypt, it took somewhat longer for a clear leader to emerge. Inscriptions found in provincial tombs of the region suggest that there was considerable jockeying for the superior position before Thebes emerged as the clear front-runner under the leadership of the nomarch Inyotef, who staked his claim to the thrones of Upper and Lower Egypt by using the traditional royal titles, by calling himself 'son of Re', and by placing his name in a cartouche. Some twenty miles to the south of Thebes, at Moalla, the tomb of Ankhtifi testifies to the struggles which had preceded the Theban triumph. Ankhtifi, nomarch of Hieraconpolis, the third Upper Egyptian nome, was in some way an ally of, or subject to, the 'kings' of Heracleopolis, and he records fighting against a coalition of Thebes and of Coptos, the region to the north of Thebes.

The poverty of surviving records prevents any coherent account of the course of events to be written. It is, however, clear that by the reign of Inyotef II, Theban power extended from Abu in the south to Tjeni in the north. Abu was the ancient name for Elephantine, which marked the southern boundary of the land of Egypt – a place to which we shall return later in this chapter. Tjeni, on the other hand, lay to the north. It was pointed out in Chapter 5 that Tjeni, more generally known by its Greek name This, was the capital of the Thinite nome in which lay Abydos. So Inyotef Wahankh controlled the six most southerly nomes of Upper Egypt, a river distance of about 235 miles to which at times the term 'Head of the South' was applied. The term, unfortunately, is rather flexible, and it is apparent that in the later Middle Kingdom it was used to embrace a rather larger stretch of territory as a specific administrative district. It is nevertheless convenient to make use of the term for our discussion in this chapter of that part of Egypt which stretches from Abydos to the beginning of the first cataract at modern Aswan. Head of the South seems a singularly appropriate appellation for this region which is in many ways so different from the rest of Upper Egypt – Middle Egypt as it is often termed – and totally unlike the Delta. Here we shall in our discussion leap-frog over Thebes which has already been separately discussed in its two important parts.

It is difficult to pin down precisely the ways in which these southern provinces of Egypt differ from those to the north. A distinct change can be sensed by the perceptive traveller, especially if he journeys by river, when he leaves Abydos (by way of Baliana), and passes through the barrage at Naga Hammadi. Shortly afterwards the Nile takes a great sweep round to the east, and for about forty miles its normal south-north flow becomes one of east-west. This is the great Qena bend, so named after the modern provincial capital that lies on the eastern end where the river again bends sharply. For the ancient Egyptians, 'to go south' was 'to go upstream'; 'to go north' was 'to go downstream'. At the Qena bend these simple directional words completely lost their meaning. The river-traveller will, however, notice the barren nature of much of the southern (locally and anciently 'western') bank of the Nile, and this possibility of no cultivated area on one or other of the river's banks becomes increasingly apparent the further south he travels, with something of a respite in the Theban area. And to the south of Luxor, the change is even more clearly marked as limestone – the prevailing rock of Egypt from Cairo southwards – gives way to sandstone. A tawny aspect invades the common outlook, becoming overpoweringly evident at Gebel es-Silsila where all cultivation ceases on both banks for a few miles, and the river cleaves its way between the rocky bluffs from which most of the best building stone was extracted from the Eighteenth Dynasty down to the Roman Period.

As a region of relative barrenness, the Head of the South is also a region of small villages and few towns of any size. It is not a region which in modern times has attracted much industry, apart from the sugar factories which process the sugar-cane from the fertile districts south of Abydos and in the neighbourhood of Luxor; although more development may be seen in hand these days, much to the displeasure of those who prefer the Egyptian countryside to be unpolluted by dark satanic mills. The impression is gained, possibly fallaciously, that nothing much happens in these southern lands to affect the attitudes of administrators in Cairo. It may be so, but in so thinking, we should not forget what has happened south of Aswan in the last twenty years with the construction of the new High Dam and all that came with it. Somehow, however, that undoubted evidence of industrial 'progress' can be forgotten as mile after mile of unsullied peaceful river bank glides past in the golden stretches which form the approach to Aswan.

There is a wealth of evidence that the Head of the South was no sleepy back-water in remote antiquity. Indeed, on the contrary, there are good reasons to locate in this part of Upper Egypt the cultural centres which in due course were to play the most important parts in the unification of Egypt and the formation of the dynastic civilisation. This,

**120** Limestone inscription containing the biographical text of Tjetji, treasurer of the kings Inyotef II and III of the Eleventh Dynasty.

however, is a hazardous claim to make, because it depends largely on what has actually been found in excavations in a part of Egypt where conditions favour survival. The unknown region of the Delta has always to be glanced at, nervously, over the shoulder when broad claims are made for Upper Egypt. It must be admitted that all one's instincts, influenced by strong ancient Egyptian traditions and some scanty discoveries, clamour for a lively Delta representation in the formative elements of the Egyptian state and Egyptian culture; but substantial discoveries are needed to reinforce these instincts.

Something has already been said in the chapter on Abydos about the traces of the early dynasties in the region, including the royal tombs excavated in the region anciently known as Poqer, and of the discoveries of predynastic graves at nearby El-Amra. It was, in fact, not very much further upstream, a few miles to the south of the eastern end of the Qena bend, that Flinders Petrie found the first great cemeteries of what are now termed the predynastic cultures. The significant region lay on the west bank of the Nile, opposite the modern village of Quft (ancient Coptos) and the modern town of Qus (ancient Apollinopolis Parva), a tract of about fifteen miles lying above the inundation level and marked at its northern end by the village of Ballas and at the south by Naqada. Here in 1894–5 Petrie came with his assistant J.E. Quibell and a few additional helpers, and the available forces were divided between Quibell at Ballas and Petrie at Naqada. Nearly 3,000 graves of very puzzling kinds were excavated. Not only were the burial customs revealed very different from what Petrie was used to from sites elsewhere in Egypt, but the pottery was equally unusual. So unusual, in fact, were the finds that Petrie postulated what he called the 'New Race', identifying it as an invading group, which most probably had entered Egypt in the chaotic First Intermediate Period. Let it be said immediately that it took almost no time for Petrie to discover his error, but not before he had published his first general findings in a volume which represents one of the classic excavation reports in the whole of Egyptology.

Before we consider the correcting of Petrie's erroneous identification of the 'New Race', it is worth glancing at another aspect of this Naqada/Ballas excavation which has had an enduring effect on excavation practices in Egypt right up to the present day. In 1893–4, Petrie had excavated on the east bank of the river at Quft and had found the local workmen peculiarly apt at picking up the skills he needed for careful, responsible excavation. In the following year at Naqada and Ballas he was able more testingly to confirm his confidence in the talents of these Quftis. In his report he describes the rigorous standards he applied, especially in the excavation of delicate skeletons:

In the first place, strict discipline was maintained among the men, and new comers were carefully allotted with old hands, so as to be educated. Carelessness in breaking up skeletons was punished, sometimes severely . . . I announced that the next man who broke bones would be dismissed . . . A rather good man was the unlucky one, and when I found two fresh fractures, he was paid up at once, and sent off. Every lad trembled in his hole after that, and was terrified if I came on even a snapped rib. In another case, where a lad tried to recompose a skeleton which he had broken up, he turned some vertebrae upside down; he was never allowed tomb-digging afterwards, and was set to the dullest and most unproductive of big holes in the town.

Petrie then gives a fairly detailed account of how he organised the work of tomb excavation and recording, in which he expressed clearly the debt he owed to his Qufti workmen. So successful were they at acquiring the necessary techniques and so

121 A timeless Nile scene in Upper Egypt.

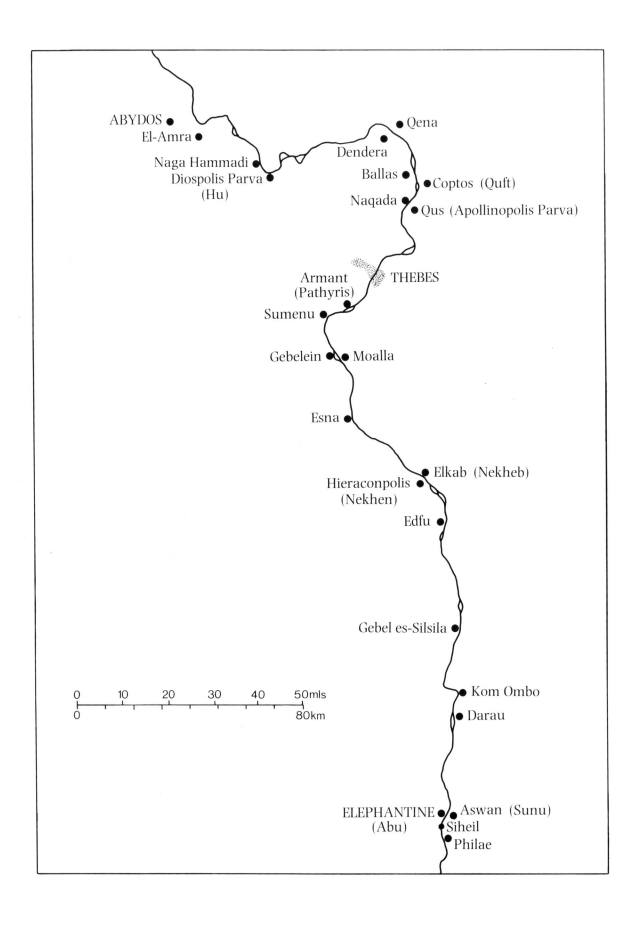

ABYDOS ●

El-Amra ●

Naga Hammadi ●
Diospolis Parva ●
(Hu)

Qena ●

Dendera ●

Ballas ●
Naqada ●

Coptos  (Quft) ●

Qus  (Apollinopolis Parva) ●

Armant ●
(Pathyris)

THEBES

Sumenu ●

Gebelein ●● Moalla

Esna ●

Elkab  (Nekheb) ●

Hieraconpolis ●
(Nekhen)

Edfu ●

Gebel es-Silsila ●

0    10    20    30    40    50mls
0                              80km

Kom Ombo ●

Darau ●

ELEPHANTINE ●● Aswan  (Sunu)
(Abu)
Siheil ●
Philae ●

trustworthy in their execution, that Petrie thereafter always used Quftis in his work in Egypt, and the practice has been adopted by most excavators who have subsequently worked in Egypt. At the present time, when the techniques of field-work have become infinitely more complex than in Petrie's day, the Qufti still has his place in any team and it is rare to visit an excavation in which the Egyptian field-workers are not supervised by a Qufti foreman or *reis*.

Huge quantities of pottery in particular were retrieved from the cemeteries at Naqada and Ballas, and were in due course to form the basic corpus of material on which the sequence of predynastic cultures was based. But the working out of a carefully organised system was not attempted by Petrie until a few years later when he excavated another large cemetery including many predynastic graves in the neighbourhood of Hu, site of the ancient town of Diospolis Parva, at the western end of the Qena bend. Having persuaded himself, on the basis of discoveries elsewhere, and by himself at Dendera, a little way up-river, that he had been wrong over the 'New Race' (although he vigorously defended his logic in reaching the conclusion he had somewhat prematurely published earlier), Petrie used the rich finds from Diospolis Parva to review his discoveries from Naqada and Ballas. The result was a remarkable system of 'sequence dates' for the stages of the predynastic cultures, extending up into the earliest dynasties, on which most subsequent work on these very early periods was based until after the Second World War. It is still common to describe the earlier stage of predynastic civilisation as the Naqada I period, and the later as Naqada II. Outside Cairo, the best representation of material from Naqada can be seen at the Ashmolean Museum, Oxford; for finds from Diospolis Parva, an excellent sample is held at the British Museum, where it can be compared with the even earlier material from what is called the Badarian culture (discussed in Chapter 4).

The 'west' bank of the Nile at Diospolis Parva – which is actually the south bank of the Qena bend – presents a very barren appearance as one passes by on the river; but the alluvial plain is more in evidence thirty miles upstream, where the great temple of Dendera stands on the desert edge, a full mile away from the river. Dedicated to the goddess Hathor, here mostly shown in human form, and not as a cow as in the Hathor shrine at Deir el-Bahri, this is the first of the surviving great temples of the Graeco-Roman Period which punctuate the progress of the traveller as he journeys through the region of the Head of the South. Dendera, Esna, Edfu, Kom Ombo, Philae, are all witnesses of the extraordinary religious building activities of the Ptolemies, the Macedonian Greek successors of Alexander the Great, and of the Roman emperors down to the third century AD. And there were others too, both in the same Head of the South district, and further to the north. At Qau el-Kebir (to the north of Akhmim), known as Antaeopolis in Graeco-Roman times, a fine Ptolemaic temple, much mentioned and engraved in the works of early travellers, was swept away by the Nile in 1821; at Armant (south of Luxor) an equally splendid temple built mainly by the great Cleopatra and Ptolemy Caesarion (her son by Julius Caesar), was dismantled in the mid-nineteenth century and used to build a new sugar factory.

There can be no doubt that substantial efforts to win the favour of the native population of Egypt were made by their Greek and Roman masters through temple building. It is, however, by no means established that these evident testimonies of the

*Left:* The Head of the South: southern Upper Egypt.

**122** *(overleaf)* An Upper Egyptian village on the east bank of the Nile.

patronage of the ancient cults by foreign rulers produced a result commensurate with the efforts involved. Probably the priestly cadres of the cults were gratified to be provided with fine new buildings; and the quarrymen, stonemasons and artists employed on the building and decoration of the same were surely pleased to have so much work to do. But the whole campaign may have been misconceived and misapplied; for there is much native evidence, some of which is certainly of a negative kind, to suggest that the great cults were already moribund. It is certain that the lavish ritual decoration and vast body of inscriptions found in these temples represent the extravagant last manifestations of a glorious tradition. There is, nevertheless, good reason to believe that the performance of the cult services in these temples and the celebration of the great festivals were regularly and properly carried out, especially the latter which, as we shall see at Edfu, provided occasions for popular carnivals.

The Dendera temple, although not as complete as Edfu, is in some ways the most satisfying monument of its kind for the visitor to inspect. True, it lacks vast pylons and a wide, imposing, first court; but it has just about everything else complete. To advance through the pronaos – the term from classical architecture which is used to describe the first hypostyle hall – followed by the inner hypostyle, and two successive vestibules, all flanked by rooms with various ritual purpose, to reach finally the totally dark sanctuary,

**123** Looking down on the *mammisi* of the Temple of Hathor at Dendera, from the roof of the pronaos of the main temple.

is a journey from light to utter darkness, a progression from the brightness of the Egyptian sun to the mystery of the holy-of-holies. Here the receptive visitor can experience something of the awe which must have attended the approach to the sanctuary by the king or his officiating priestly deputy in the high days of Egyptian civilisation. Even now, when crowds of tourists arrive and flood the temple with an urgent desire to see all in a short hour or so, it is possible to find a corner where contemplation of the past can be practised under the gaze (when the face and eyes are not mutilated) of the gods, kings and priests who people every available space on the temple walls. The temple also preserves on its roof two little chapels for special ceremonies, for Hathor, the temple's own special deity, and for Osiris. To reach them by a long shallow stair on the east side of the building, or by another on the west side winding around a square stair-well, is to follow the paths of the priestly processions which accompany the visitor in relief carvings on the walls. One ascends with the priests, shuffling up the shallow treads, weighed down in imagination by the ritual vessels, boxes and standards carried in procession on an important day of festival.

In the temple enclosure at Dendera, a fine sacred pool lay on the west side of the main building. It no longer holds water, and its appearance is nicely embellished with a palm tree and other greenery. Occasionally a donkey may be found grazing on the damp floor of the pool; it has descended one of the well-preserved stairways to sample the lush pasture which, no doubt, still retains a trace of its former holy essence. A last building may also be noticed, the small, perfectly preserved, structure of a kind called by Egyptologists *mammisi*. A *mammisi* is found as an adjunct to all the great late temples. The word *mammisi* itself is a coinage of the great Champollion, using his knowledge of the Coptic language, to describe the 'birth-house' in which the birth of the child member of the temple triad or family of gods was celebrated, and by magical association, the divine birth of the Egyptian king himself. The *mammisi* at Dendera, a small temple in its own right, commemorates the birth of Ihy, the child of Hathor 'mistress of Dendera' and her local consort Hor-smatawy (Horus who unites the Two Lands).

The scenes within, which represent the divine courtship of the parents, the formation of the child Ihy and his *ka* or spirit by the god Khnum on a potter's wheel, the attendance of 'midwife' deities, male and female, the birth and presentation of the infant, and other ceremonies connected with the great event, all find their origins in the Eighteenth Dynasty. Hatshepsut, whose claim to the throne was recognisably shaky, presented herself as a child of Amon-Re in what may be regarded as the prototype series of scenes in the temple at Deir el-Bahri. Amenophis III, with less pressing reasons, set aside a whole room for the same purpose in the temple of Luxor. In the Graeco-Roman Period, the need for justification was apparently felt especially strongly by the foreign rulers, the latter-day 'Pharaohs' of Macedon and Rome. But the fashion seems to have been revived by King Nectanebo I, who himself erected the first known purpose-built *mammisi* at Dendera, near the place where the later building just described was constructed. Nectanebo I (380–362 BC) of the Thirtieth Dynasty, although recognised as one of the last native Egyptian rulers, owed his royal position to political, rather than hereditary, forces, and may have felt that some extra justification had to be provided to establish his legitimacy.

About fifteen miles upstream from Dendera, and on the eastern bank of the Nile, at a

123

124 A watercolour by Sir John G. Wilkinson of a device for raising water in the neighbourhood of Coptos; it is a *saqiya*, or water-wheel driven by animals, first used in Egypt in the Ptolemaic Period.

stretch of the river which runs almost directly due north before it turns sharply left into the Qena bend, lies the town of Quft, the source of Petrie's skilled excavators and the site of the ancient town of Gebtiu, known to the Greeks as Coptos. Here is a good and clear case of the ancient name being continued and preserved in the modern form: Gebtiu → Coptos → Quft (allowing for the phonetic similarties of G, C (or K in Greek) and Q, and of B, P and F). The principal deity of the place was Min, the god of human fertility, among other attributes, who was commonly represented in a permanent state of sexual excitement, who was also the principal deity of Akhmim in Middle Egypt, and who was closely assimilated to the great imperial god Amon-Re of Luxor. It might be expected that

125 A procession with musicians in festive mood advances to a shrine of Hathor: a scene carved on the outside of a steatite bowl.

178

rites of a particularly orgiastic kind might have been celebrated at Coptos, but ancient sources are disappointingly silent in this respect.

It is known that Min-festivals occupied important places in the religious calendar of ancient Egypt; there are regular mentions of the 'going-forth of Min' festival in tombs of the Old Kingdom; there are many references to, and some representations of, the great Min harvest-festival, celebrated in association with Amon-Re, at Luxor during the New Kingdom. In the latter festival it was the fertility of the land in particular that was celebrated, although the idea of fertility in general lay not far beneath the surface. Among the ritual acts performed at this time, on the eve of the new moon at the start of the harvest season, were the cutting by the king of a token sheaf of grain and the leading of a white bull in procession. The bull was ever a potent symbol of fertility in ancient Egypt, the sheaf of grain was the evident result of fertility to be offered to the deity. But what about Coptos itself?

A charming and perhaps suggestive record of unbuttoned celebrations seems to be preserved on a steatite (soap-stone) bowl, which, from internal evidence, may have come originally from Coptos. The evidence is contained in two lines of text carved in the demotic script, the cursive form of writing used generally in Egypt for non-formal purposes from the seventh century BC down to the fifth century AD. It states: 'In the presence of the Lord of Coptos, the Great God, from the hand of the servant Petearpocrates son of Esthotes'. The text is a relatively commonplace dedication, in this case of the bowl presented to the Lord of Coptos, almost certainly Min, by Petearpocrates, who describes himself deferentially as 'servant'. On the basis of the style of the demotic script, and of details in the scene, which we shall now look at, the piece may be dated to about 525–500 BC.

The subject of the low relief scene is a procession moving towards a shrine, here represented by a typical Hathor-head – full-faced with cow's ears, heavy wig with curled ends, and a vestigial sistrum-headdress on top – flanked by stumpy papyrus-columns. This shrine is further flanked by bushes on which long-horned antelopes or oryxes apparently graze. The antelope/oryx on the left also leads the procession which approaches the shrine. A bull comes next, partly kneeling as if about to be offered in sacrifice; then five people who provide music and many additional points of interest; they all sport lotus-flowers on the tops of their heads. The first, who wears a fringed tunic

(possibly a Persian innovation), beats a small circular tambourine or drum; the second, similarly dressed, plucks at a lyre; the third, who shuffles forward with some indication of sinuous movement, wears a longer tunic and is probably female; she wields a pair of clappers. The fourth person, heavy-hipped, is also probably a woman, and she is the most interesting of all. She seems to hold her hitched up garment with her left hand, and, bending forward to present a better target, she strikes her buttock with her right hand. She can only be providing a rhythmical accompaniment to the music of her companions, a variant to the hand-clapping which is so often shown in tomb-scenes of musical entertainment and which is such a regular feature of simple singing in Egypt today. It is also possible to put a somewhat more lubricious interpretation on the episode, bringing to mind Herodotus' description of the excesses performed at the great festival of Bubastis in late Pharaonic times (see Chapter 1). It seems rather tame to note that the fifth member of the party, bringing up the rear, wears a traditional Egyptian triangular kilt, and plays a descant on his double pipes.

Leap-frogging Luxor, our progress southwards passes by a region which shows every sign of having been extensively populated in antiquity, with substantial remains of predynastic and early-dynastic cemeteries, of shrines and settlements of the dynastic period, and of lively Greek cities in the Ptolemaic and Roman Periods. Armant and its sugar factory have already been mentioned. Here also was a famous bull-cult, similar to, but less influential than that of the Memphite Apis. The Bucchis-bull was likewise selected according to specific markings, and buried in subterranean tombs of elaborate construction. The cult flourished especially under the Roman emperors. Beyond Armant, a little further south, is the ancient site of Sumenu, of considerable importance in the Middle Kingdom and later as having an important cult of the crocodile-god Sobk; and then comes Gebelein, a place where significant discoveries from both ends of the ancient historical spectrum have been made, in particular large quantities of papyrus documents dating from the Ptolemaic and Roman Periods when the old town-name of Per-Hathor was reshaped into the classical form Pathyris. But perhaps no discovery from the Gebelein region is so well known as the late predynastic body in the British Museum, which for generations has been affectionately called Ginger because of the substantial remains of tawny-coloured hair still preserved on his head. Wallis Budge, who instituted the small excavation which produced this sad relic, and a number of other similar, but less well preserved bodies, was unusually pleased that he had succeeded in adding such a fine example of a body, desiccated but not mummified (in the strict sense of the word), to the very representative collections in London. A subsequently fabricated scandalous rumour that Ginger was not a predynastic body, but a modern Egyptian (even the brother of the Luxor antiquities dealer who had organised the excavation) suitably treated, has happily been wholly discredited by a Carbon-14 test. Ginger is very old; and he now has a certificate to prove the fact.

Some forty miles south of Luxor, the character of the landscape on both sides of the river begins to develop an austerity of appearance which suggests barrenness, remoteness, lack of population; villages become sparser and smaller. There is a feeling of isolation, a sense of nothing much having happened in recent years, or indeed for the last few thousand years. And yet, just here were two of the most important places in Upper Egypt in remote antiquity. Here on the east bank, where there is scarcely an acre of

126 Stela from Armant, dated to 296 AD in the reign of Diocletian, showing a mummified Bucchis bull receiving worship from the emperor.

127 *(far right)* Demotic letter from Gebelein, written by Petesukhos to his brother in 95 BC, enquiring after the health of various members of their family.

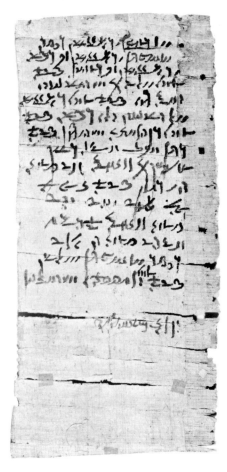

cultivation, was the city of Nekheb (modern Elkab), the home of the cult of Nekhbet, the vulture-goddess who was the tutelary deity – the protective deity – of the King of Upper Egypt. And opposite, across the Nile on the west bank, but about half a mile inland across a district of modest cultivation, lie the scanty remains of the city and necropolis of Nekhen, home of a very important cult of the falcon-god Horus, and more generally known as Hieraconpolis (Falcon City). A wealth of evidence points to the importance of Hieraconpolis in very early times, and it is commonly believed that the Upper Egyptian coalition of provinces which secured the upper hand over a Lower Egyptian coalition and imposed unity on the whole land of Egypt had its springs of power in this southern city. It was at Hieraconpolis, for example, that the Narmer palette, the most famous early monument, perhaps even document, was found. Precious remains of a very early painted tomb, probably of the latest predynastic times, were found here; equally, huge deposits of remarkable carved ivories, the quality and interest of which are only now being properly appreciated. Excellently conserved examples can be seen in the Ashmolean Museum, Oxford, and in the Petrie Museum at University College London.

128 Late predynastic body from the cemetery of Gebelein: a corpse desiccated by the hot sand, not a mummy. The grave goods surrounding the body were not found with it, but are typical of contemporary burials.

129 The house built for himself at Elkab by Somers Clarke, now used as an excavation headquarters by Belgian Egyptologists.

There can be no doubt from what has been found in this desperately disturbed and plundered site that this region was no sleepy backwater 5,000 years ago.

Nekheb on the other side of the river, although clearly a twin of Hieraconpolis, was in no way as important in the earliest period, in spite of the presence of the cult-centre of Nekhbet. It subsequently achieved greater local significance as the capital of the third Upper Egyptian nome, while the capital of the second nome on the west bank, in which Hieraconpolis lay, was Edfu, also the centre of an important falcon cult. Nekheb (Elkab) is best known generally for its huge town enclosure, a massive mud-brick fortification with walls over twelve metres thick, dating probably from the later Dynastic Period, and also for a series of rock-cut tombs, mostly of Eighteenth-Dynasty date, containing informative scenes of daily life enlivened by the casual comments of the various men and women who are taking part in the posthumous activities of the tomb-owners. It is a site where the essential humanity of the ancient Egyptians is brought fully to one's consciousness. Small wonder, then, that Somers Clarke, architect and archaeologist, who did so much to rescue and protect the antiquities of Elkab – to say nothing of his tireless work in the cause of restoration and conservation elsewhere in Egypt and Nubia – chose to settle in a fine house on the Nile's edge at the southern end of the ancient site; and there he eventually died and was buried. The house is still used regularly as a dig-house by Belgian excavators working in Elkab.

About twenty miles south of Hieraconpolis and Elkab lies the town of Edfu, an ancient settlement which is now visited chiefly for the huge, and almost completely preserved, temple dedicated to Horus of Behdet, the sacred falcon. The approach to the temple precinct is usually undertaken in old-fashioned horsedrawn carriages, driven with wild indifference for horse, vehicle and occupants, by cabbies whose first aim is to reach the finishing-post at the temple before the rest of the field, so as to hurtle back to the river-bank for the next fare. The quiet of the temple precinct follows gratefully the pandemonium at the entrance where the milling of carriages and the shouts of cabbies

129

mingle with the urgent solicitations of the proprietors of the booths which have in recent years been allowed to develop as a kind of open-air bazaar.

130 Much can be learned from the wealth of texts which smother the walls of the temple about the ceremonies which took place at regular intervals throughout the year within and without the sacred precinct. And from some specially informative inscriptions the events of certain festivals are set out in great detail, and some indication is given of how the populace in general was able to participate. The most interesting festival occurred in the third month of the summer season, beginning on the first day – the day of the new moon – and ending on the day of the full moon. It was built around a visit made by Hathor of Dendera to Horus of Edfu, in the course of which a marriage took place between the two deities. At times there is something quite cosy about the divinities of ancient Egypt, especially when they are shown engaged in domestic activities. They were very inclined to visit one another, to spend some time in neighbouring or even distant shrines; the epithet 'visiting' was frequently applied to a god who might be met in a strange context, spending a brief vacation with another god. So Hathor moved out of Dendera two weeks in advance of the new moon, her glittering procession of boats moving steadily upstream, stopping frequently at intervening shrines to pay her respects, and to give her priestly retinue opportunities for a series of entertainments and much hospitality.

The reception of the goddess at the quay at Edfu, precisely at the eighth daylight hour of the first day of the month, was a brilliant and clamorous occasion and one may envisage the progress as Horus conducted her to his temple, with the ancient predecessors of the Edfu cabbies jockeying for favoured positions in the crush which accompanied the main procession. The actual sacred marriage took place early in the proceedings, and most of the festival was taken up with more processions and ceremonies, some of which went some distance out of the temple precinct. On such occasions the ordinary people could enter briefly into the religious life of a great temple, and participate in the activities of the cult. An Edfu text describes the richness and grandeur of the temple, to be seen quite clearly at such a time:

Its supplies are more abundant than the sands of the shore . . . wine flows in the districts like the inundation pouring from the Two Caverns; myrrh is on the fire and incense can be smelt a mile away. It is decorated with faience, shining with natron, decked with flowers and herbs. The priests and officiants are dressed in fine linen; the king's party is made fine in its regalia; its young people are drunk; its populace is happy; its young girls are beautiful to see; jollity is all around it; carnival is in all its districts; there is no sleep there until dawn.

Edfu and the other great temples of Upper Egypt, including most of those built during the New Kingdom at Thebes, were constructed from the fine sandstone which forms the hills in this region of the Nile. The best stone was extracted from a series of quarries extending south from Edfu down to Gebel es-Silsila, twenty-five miles away. Many of the quarries, which can easily be seen from the river, the neat traces of ancient stone-extraction being clearly visible to the naked eye, seem small and scarcely worth working. But close inspection shows how economically the rock faces were worked; the best use was made of whatever stone seemed suitable for exploitation. Modern quarrying with dynamite, which is also carried on in the same region, is profligate and excessively wasteful by comparison with ancient practice, which can be best observed in the incredibly lofty and extensive quarries at Gebel es-Silsila itself. Here the Nile is hedged in by low hills on east and west, and it is thought that at one time there might have been a series of rapids which were difficult to negotiate especially at the time of the inundation.

The most imposing quarries are on the east bank of the river, approached by a narrow defile along which the cut stone was drawn down to the port where barges could be loaded. A mass of inscriptions, mostly the hasty scribbles of workmen and casual visitors in antiquity, are to be seen on the quarried faces of the rock, but two more formal records may be mentioned: one set up in the early reign of Akhenaten, before he moved his capital to El-Amarna, recording the cutting of stone for the Aten temples at Karnak; the other, less imposing but still significant, recording the re-opening of the quarries in the early twentieth century for the extraction of stone to build the great Nile barrage at Esna. On the west bank, however, is a series of monuments, inscriptions, shrines, and a small rock-cut temple, which point to the existence of a lively cult of the Nile deities at this place in the New Kingdom. Those high officials who came there to supervise or observe the quarrying were surely impressed by the power of the Nile at flood-time and felt the divine presence of the appropriate deity, Hapy. It is still a place of strange attraction and fascination; it is remote – no village can be seen – it is little visited; it is full of the ghosts of the past, of quarrymen, of great officials like Hatshepsut's Senenmut, whose shrine was systematically defaced in antiquity, of King Horemheb whose small temple is itself an archive in stone of interesting inscriptions. And at the south end, near the great Nile inscriptions of Sethos I, Ramesses II and Merenptah, is the extraordinary 'capstan' a huge misshapen piece of rock rather like an anvil, set on a pillar which was clearly left after the stone all around had been quarried away. Here, as legend has it, was fastened one end of the great rope or chain slung across the Nile in medieval times to prevent or control the passage of boats.

From Gebel es-Silsila to Aswan the river runs between mostly barren land on one or both sides. There is some lush cultivation in the neighbourhood of Kom Ombo, where the great double temple of the crocodile Sobk and the falcon Haroeris stands high above the river. Generally, however, the journey provides a foretaste of Nubia with yellow sand dunes pouring down the hills towards the river, especially on the west side. It is right to think of Nubia in this stretch of river, because ethnically the population of Egypt changes from about the village of Darau, a few miles to the south of Kom Ombo. Traditionally, Darau marked the boundary between Arabic- and Nubian-speaking Egyptians. The preponderance of Nubian speakers was declining until the construction of the High Dam, when the great majority of Egyptian Nubians from the flooded region south of the Dam were moved and resettled in the Wadi Kom Ombo and the neighbouring districts.

So Aswan is approached, and the southern boundary of Egypt reached. In antiquity there were fairly precise ideas about what was Egypt and what could be termed foreign parts. The exact boundary lay just south of the modern town of Aswan, the site of ancient Sunu (in Greek Syene), for it was to the south, according to legend that the Nile poured forth from the caverns in the cataract. Throughout Egyptian history no attempt was made to extend Egypt's boundaries further south. There was, as it seems, a finite extent to the land of Egypt; and it would probably have seemed quite improper, if not blasphemous, to include what once was foreign territory into the sacred motherland.

Until the very late Pharaonic Period, the main town in this outpost was on the island

130 (left) The great formal pylon of the Ptolemaic temple at Edfu dedicated to Horus. The scenes of the king smiting his enemies may be compared with that on the ivory tablet of King Den, in fig. 74.

131 (left) Painted niche in the chapel of the rock-cut tomb of the nomarch Sirenput II at Qubbet el-Hawa, opposite Aswan. The tomb-owner, here called Nubkaurenakhte, receives offerings from his son.

132 (right) The fortified Coptic monastery of St Simeon in the desert west of Aswan. The view looks from the church to the upper level which contains the living quarters of the monks.

in the river opposite Sunu. Here was Elephantine, as the Greeks called it; Abu to the Egyptians, as we saw at the very beginning of this chapter. The word Abu in Egyptian means both 'ivory' and 'elephant', and much discussion has taken place over the significance and origin of the name. There is plenty of room for speculation: the town on the island was an emporium for the ivory trade; it was a place where elephants might be seen; the island's shape looked like an elephant wallowing in the river; the smooth black rocks of the cataract also looked like elephants. There is no way of settling the matter, but it is not insignificant that the Greeks chose to call the island Elephantine. The link with that noble animal was clearly well established by the time when Greeks were in a position in Egypt to start naming places for themselves. From elsewhere it is patently evident that they were in the habit of picking very apposite Greek names, which indicate, generally speaking, a fair understanding of the ancient Egyptian names.

134    The settlement on Elephantine island was certainly large and influential from the time of the early Old Kingdom down to the late New Kingdom; it retained some importance later, and was undoubtedly a major political centre in the Graeco-Roman Period when there was a marked revival of interest in the land of Nubia to the south. The nomarchs of this first Upper-Egyptian nome achieved very particular power during the Old Kingdom, when the very distance from Memphis and the royal Residence allowed them much greater freedom of action than their nomarch colleagues further north. The tombs of these local governors, sited dramatically in the hill of Qubbet el-Hawa, overlooking the north end of Elephantine, point unequivocally to their relative independence as the king's representatives on the sensitive southern boundary. The decorations in these

131    tombs are often gauche – pejoratively described as provincial – but the inscriptions reveal what freedom of action was allowed to these nomarchs in the conduct of expeditions to the south. No record is more appealing than that of Harkhuf, which includes a transcript of the letter he received from his young monarch Pepi II, commending him for having brought back a dwarf for his Majesty from one of his Nubian forays: nothing pleased the king more, and he urges Harkhuf to take the utmost care of his trophy until he can bring it to the Residence.

Near the tomb of Harkhuf is the complicated tomb of a commander of foreign troops called Heqaib, who exercised his important office also in the reign of Pepi II of the Sixth Dynasty. Heqaib is of special interest because he became the subject of a local cult practised during the early Middle Kingdom in a shrine on Elephantine island. Since the Second World War remarkable sculptures have been found associated with this shrine, some of which may be seen in the Aswan Museum on the same island. One black granite torso, which is so similar in style to these statues that it is now commonly thought to have been made in the same workshops at this southern provincial capital, has been in

133    London since the early nineteenth century. The head is very strongly modelled, and the eyes were inlaid – a technique not commonly used for hard stone sculptures in the Middle Kingdom.

A royal sculpture which is known to have come from Elephantine shows Ramesses II wearing a tight wig and the double crown, and holding the royal regalia, the crook and flail. It was presented to the British Museum in 1838 by William Hamilton, who had commented so shrewdly on the Younger Memnon bust thirty years earlier. The exact provenance of this sculpture is not known, but its local origin is confirmed not only by

133 Black granite bust of a man, originally with inlaid eyes. A strong portrait in the manner of Elephantine sculpture of the Middle Kingdom.

134 (overleaf) View of the remains of the city mound on the island of Elephantine, showing the levels of successive occupation revealed in the course of excavation.

189

Hamilton's description in his *Aegyptiaca* of 1809 but also by the inscriptions on the back-pillar in which the local divine triad of Khnum, Anukis and Satis is mentioned. Elephantine, in spite of its known historical importance, has until recently received very little attention from archaeologists, partly because much of the ancient mound was occupied by modern villages. The picture is now beginning to change, as extensive excavation by the German Archaeological Institute begins to probe the lower levels. Much will be learned in the coming years.

The activity which made the region so important in antiquity was closely related to what was happening to the south in Nubia. Some aspects of the history and geography of the region are therefore reserved for the next chapter. But before the transition is made, let us cross the Nile to the west bank, skirting the small Kitchener Island with its splendid botanical gardens. Landing on the river-bank we may take either the desert path up the deep *wadi* leading to the west, or the made-up path which rises steeply to the impressive mausoleum of the Aga Khan which commands one of the heights overlooking the Nile and the first cataract. Whichever path we take, the goal is to be the monastery of St Simeon, set in the desert not quite one mile from the river. Here, in what once was splendid isolation, a great fortified religious community was founded in the seventh century. It was abandoned in the thirteenth century, but so well preserved and so successfully restored are many of the buildings, that even today Sunday masses in the Coptic rite are still occasionally celebrated. The complex within the substantial enclosure wall contains all the characteristic features of a Coptic monastery, built on two levels, as the conformation of the ground demands. Here may be seen the cells of the monks, their refectory, kitchen, their church, their camel-park and their sanitary arrangements – friendly multiple-seaters. To come here at a quiet time impresses the thoughtful visitor with a strong sense of peace. Although the place seems remote, it is in fact but a short distance from the river and the towns of Elephantine and Aswan. Nevertheless, it was a successful retreat for about six hundred years, and offered a spiritual contrast to the active, bustling life of the African emporium which for so many millennia had been the function of the southernmost city of Egypt proper.

132

# CHAPTER NINE

# Land of Outposts

## NUBIA

A FEW MILES to the south of Aswan, in the middle of the cataract-fractured flow of the Nile, rises the island of Siheil. It is a pleasant morning's sail from Aswan if the wind is right, and as a terminus for an excursion it is very rewarding, not least because it is not commonly visited. One is immediately struck by the large number of inscriptions on the tumbled granite rocks and outcrops which make up the island. How different are these from what one expects an Egyptian inscription to be! They are not conventionally carved, but bruised on the granite, showing up in a lighter colour against the much more weathered surface of the stone itself. They are for the most part brief records set up by officials involved in expeditions to the south, or sent to supervise such foreign enterprises. Some are rather carelessly done – try bruising granite to form hieroglyphic signs – some are quite carefully executed; they show scenes of adoration of the cataract deities, name the kings in whose reigns the operations took place, and the officials principally involved. The information they contain is rarely detailed or even specific about actual expeditions, but *en masse* they indicate a wealth of activity especially during the Twelfth Dynasty and throughout the New Kingdom; and they demonstrate the strong local devotion to the triad of cataract deities, to Khnum, ram-headed, whose main shrine was on Elephantine island, to his divine wife, Anukis, distinguished by a high feathered headdress, and their daughter Satis, whose cap, rather like the white crown, was embellished with antelope horns. Both the divine ladies were specially worshipped on Siheil.

Inscriptions of the kind found on Siheil can also be seen throughout the district extending from Aswan to the southern end of the cataract; but Siheil is the most convenient place to study them in quantity, as it is the best place to consider the nature of the cataract itself. If you climb to the top of one of the pair of hills which dominate the island, you gain an excellent view over the cataract region – a kind of rocky desolation where the course of the great river is broken up into many channels by the outcrops of granite. At the present time it looks quiet and unadventurous; but in the days before the Nile was dammed a mile or two further south, and then, and more decisively, controlled again by the High Dam, the flow of the river boiled and tumbled over and around the rocks, rendering all navigation hazardous. Even at the time of inundation, the many submerged reefs presented insuperable difficulties to the skilled local navigators. Techniques to overcome the rapids were developed in the nineteenth century to haul the boats of travellers by stages from one stretch of clear water to another. Much was made of the difficulties and the need for *bakshish* was constantly emphasised. Amelia Edwards

135

**135** *(overleaf)* Part of the rocky hills on the island of Siheil. Many of the granite surfaces carry ancient records of official visits and dedications to the gods of the region.

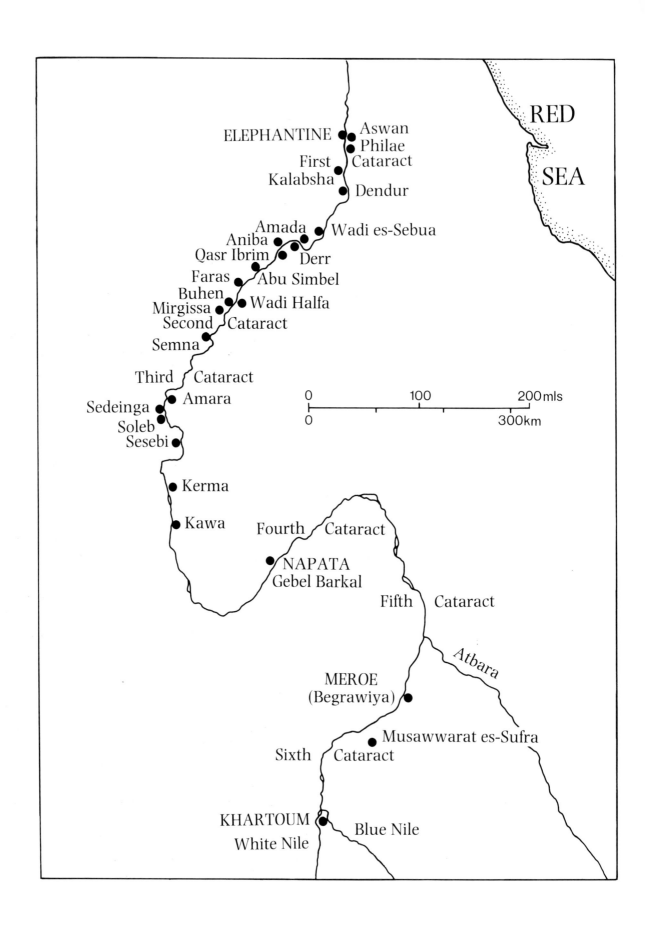

RED

SEA

ELEPHANTINE ● ● Aswan
● Philae
First Cataract
Kalabsha
● Dendur

Amada ● Wadi es-Sebua
Aniba ●
Qasr Ibrim ● Derr
Faras ● Abu Simbel
Buhen
Mirgissa ● ● Wadi Halfa
Second Cataract
Semna

Third Cataract

Sedeinga ● Amara
Soleb
Sesebi ●

● Kerma

● Kawa
Fourth Cataract

● NAPATA
Gebel Barkal
Fifth Cataract

Atbara

MEROE
(Begrawiya) ●

● Musawwarat es-Sufra
Sixth Cataract

KHARTOUM ●
White Nile Blue Nile

0        100        200 mls
0              300 km

was at the same time enraged, terrified and amused by the progress of her boat, the *Philae:*

The scene that followed was curious enough. Two ropes were carried from the dahabeeyah to the nearest island, and there made fast to the rocks. Two ropes from the island were also brought on board the dahabeeyah. A double file of men on deck, and another double file on shore, then ranged themselves along the ropes; the Sheykh gave the signal; and to a wild chanting accompaniment and a movement like a barbaric Sir Roger de Coverley dance, a system of double hauling began, by means of which the huge boat slowly and steadily ascended. We may have been a quarter of an hour going up the incline; though it seemed much longer. Meanwhile, as they warmed to their work, the men chanted louder and pulled harder, till the boat went in at last with a rush, and swung over into a pool of comparatively smooth water.

In ancient times navigation through the cataract region was no less difficult, and in spite of attempts made during the Twelfth Dynasty to cut a clear channel for shipping, it was never an easy matter to negotiate the rapids. What procedures were used is not known but they were probably not very different from those described by Miss Edwards. It is small wonder that the ancient Egyptians regarded the cataract as the southern terminus of Egypt proper. It was the first serious obstacle to navigation on the journey south from the Delta. That there were five further rocky barriers or cataracts impeding the river's flow in its more southerly reaches down to what is now the city of Khartoum was scarcely a matter of concern in early times; but from the Middle Kingdom onwards Egyptians travelling south would become very familiar with the second cataract and to a lesser extent with the third and fourth cataracts.

To travel south from Elephantine was always an adventure, and to return safely as far as the cataract region was ever a matter for congratulation. A charming story, *The Shipwrecked Sailor*, preserved on a papyrus of the Middle Kingdom in Moscow, begins with the arrival at Egypt's southern boundary of an expedition, the leader of which is depressed, apparently at his lack of success; he is bothered about what kind of reception he will get when he reports to the king. His attendant tries to cheer him up:

Buck up, Count! We are home again. The mallet is taken, the mooring-peg struck fast, the bow-warp is fixed on land. Thanks are given and god has been praised. Everyone embraces his companion. Our crew has come back safely; our expedition has suffered no loss. We have reached the end of Wawat [a part of northern Nubia], and passed by Senmut [the island of Biga]. See! We are come back in peace, we have reached our land.

The attendant concentrates on the happy circumstances of the return home, and points out, in effect, that to be back in Egypt is far more important than what may lie ahead for his master. How often must the nomarchs of Elephantine during the Old Kingdom have felt such relief when the rocky barrier of the cataract was reached! Up until the Middle Kingdom, and from time to time in later periods, an expedition south was by necessity a punitive venture. And yet the need to obtain raw materials obliged the Egyptians, probably on a very regular basis, to send expeditions at least as far as the second cataract. Gold was extracted from mines in the eastern desert, and places for the processing of ore have been found at Faras just south of the Egyptian-Sudanese border. Copper was also worked in the same region, and remains of a settlement where ore was smelted have been found near Buhen in the neighbourhood of Wadi Halfa. Fine stones for sculpture and semi-precious stones for jewellery were extracted in the western desert, and there is

Nubia from the First Cataract to Khartoum.

no reason to doubt that other useful raw materials were exploited from various sites in the same region. Where inscriptional evidence has given little indication, archaeology has occasionally identified significant sources. Sadly much of the land close to the river has now been flooded beyond archaeological investigation by the waters of what is now called Lake Nasser. Yet exploration in the hilly districts still above the water's level may reveal further traces of the pioneer exploitative activities of the ancient Egyptians.

Much more besides came through Nubia to Egypt from the south, and in particular from equatorial Africa. The trade routes which were still followed until the nineteenth century represent the channels by which exotic products reached Egypt. Traditionally these goods were shown in tomb and temple scenes in which the power and influence of the Pharaoh over foreign lands were depicted through the presentation of tribute. A good representative selection is shown in two fragments of mural painting from the Eighteenth-Dynasty Theban tomb of Sobkhotpe. Black African porters carry ebony logs, giraffe-tails (for the best fly-whisks), leopard-skins (for priestly garments), monkeys and baboons, material for eye-paint, incense, shafts for spears (difficult to obtain in Egypt from native trees), and gold made up into rings and rough nuggets for easy transport. Scenes elsewhere show that ivory was also included in the trade of such caravans, as well as other live animals – giraffes and leopards – and ostrich-feathers (for fans).

Trade through Nubia flourished in those periods when life in metropolitan Egypt was in a settled condition, and it is noticeable how the establishment, or re-establishment, of such conditions in the Twelfth and Eighteenth Dynasties was accompanied by a strong revival of trade links with the south. It is all too clear that it required impetus and organisation from the highest authority to carry forward foreign projects; and so not only in Nubia but also in the eastern desert, and Sinai, and into Asia and to the land of Punt (probably Somalia). In the southern enterprises the great officials of the first nome of Upper Egypt were deeply involved in the Old and Middle Kingdoms. From the Eighteenth Dynasty and throughout the New Kingdom, when a more concentrated effort was made to control the lands to the south, a very important official called King's Son of Kush was appointed to manage Nubian affairs. Kush was the name which emerged during the Second Intermediate Period for the region of Lower Nubia lying between the first and second cataracts, and it was used subsequently for this same region with extensions further south as far, no doubt, as the actual limit of the authority of the King's Son of Kush at any time. This official was in a very real sense the royal deputy in Nubia (and also at times the southern district of Upper Egypt) and he is commonly called Viceroy of Kush.

The whole of Lower Nubia, as it was in antiquity, settled and cultivated (where it was possible), with a substantial population, many towns and villages, and a great many monumental reminders of Egyptian occupation in the way of temples, tombs and fortresses, has now disappeared beneath the waters of Lake Nasser. The process of destruction began with the building of the first Aswan Dam between 1898 and 1912. The resulting lake which collected to the south of this huge barrage flooded most of the ancient sites and most of the temples as far south as (but not including) Abu Simbel. During the summer flood, the sluices of the dam were opened and the waters of the lake were allowed to pour through to bring the annual inundation to the land of Egypt; at this time the submerged temples rose again out of the waters. Two later heightenings of this first dam led to further losses of ancient sites, but the losses were not to be compared with what was threatened by the building of the new High Dam (Sadd el'Ali) in the 1960s. Then the lake to the south would be permanent, with no annual opening of sluices. This threat led to what was undoubtedly the greatest of international archaeological campaigns to save the monuments of Nubia. Not only was every kind of surviving site investigated, the region ransacked for unidentified settlements, and careful records made of all inscriptions, formal and informal (including graffiti) carved or scratched on rocks and immovable monuments, but all the free-standing temples and other ancient buildings capable of being moved were transferred to new sites on higher ground, or even sent abroad as gifts to countries that had been specially generous in their help. A few rock-cut temples and tombs were also moved – in the case of the Abu Simbel temples the task of moving was in itself a project of heroic effort both financial and engineering.

In general, our progress south to the second cataract and beyond must ignore what has happened during the twentieth century AD, but some reference will have to be made from time to time to recent events, especially where monuments may have been relocated and can still be seen. We are at once faced with this need to be anachronistic when the island of Philae is reached. When the expedition mentioned in *The Shipwrecked*

136 *(below left)* The obelisk from the temple of Philae standing in the park at Kingston Lacy, Dorset.

137 A scene from the tomb of Sobkhotpe, showing porters bringing the products of tropical Africa, including gold, ebony, leopard skins, giraffe tails, a monkey and a baboon.

*Sailor* reached the Egyptian frontier, it was described as having 'reached the end of Wawat, and passed Senmut'. Senmut, the island now named Biga, was famed in antiquity as being the site of the *abaton*, the 'unapproachable' place where Osiris was buried, and nearby were the two great mythical caverns from which the Nile traditionally poured forth. Close to Biga lay the island of Philae, on which a great temple complex dedicated to Isis was constructed in the Ptolemaic and Roman Periods.

139

In the days of the shipwrecked sailor's arrival at Senmut, the island was, it seems, unoccupied by any noble structure, and may even have had no name. Today the island is equally of no consequence; for it can no longer be seen, its position alone marked by the top of the coffer dam which surrounded it while its buildings were dismantled, to be transferred to the neighbouring island of Agilkia. The move was necessary because after the construction of the High Dam, Philae island and its temple were trapped in the waters of the lake which lay between the old and the new dams. Fluctuations in the water level of this lake would in time have had a disastrous effect on the temple, and drastic action was needed to save it by moving it to Agilkia. So now Agilkia has become Philae, and so it will be called by all who visit it, to be charmed by the buildings and the setting. And when the trees and shrubs are well established it will surely once again become the 'Pearl of Egypt', as it was to nineteenth century travellers.

138

In the moving of the buildings from the old island of Philae to Agilkia, very great care was taken to shape the latter so as to resemble the former as closely as possible and to ensure that when the temple complex was rebuilt it should be oriented in its new site precisely as it had been in its old. The highly successful outcome of the operation now enables the temple and its subsidiary buildings to be visited and examined in a way that has not been possible for nearly a century. There was a time during the year when the Aswan dam sluices were opened and the water level fell sufficiently to permit visitors to walk about the old island; but the temple buildings were greatly encumbered with mud, and 'a stroll through the courts coincided with the hottest time of the year when temperatures well above 40°C would be common for much of the day. For most of the year, however, no access was possible except occasionally by water when the level of the lake allowed a small rowing boat to pass beneath the heavy lintels into the temple courts. Such a visit might have been romantic, but it mostly served to impress on the visitor the tragedy of the temple's plight. How much better it is now, especially as the move has allowed the reconstruction of several small buildings and the replacing of fallen blocks – the casualties of nearly two thousand years of neglect.

136

One monument from Philae may now, rather unexpectedly, be found in the park of Kingston Lacy House near Wimborne in Dorset. It is an obelisk, about 22 feet high above its pedestal – small by Egyptian standards – which was originally one of a pair placed in front of the first pylon of the main temple. It was brought to Dorset by William John Bankes, to whom it had been given by Henry Salt. This obelisk and its base played a not unimportant part in the early history of the decipherment of hieroglyphs, but they almost escaped playing this role through a serious misfortune at the time of removal from the island. The obelisk had first been noted by Belzoni in 1816 during the return from his initial journey up the Nile to Abu Simbel. He laid claim to it in the name of Henry Salt on the basis of the blanket permission to remove antiquities granted by Muhammad Ali, Pasha of Egypt. He made no attempt to move it until two years later when he travelled in some style from Thebes to Aswan in the company of Henry Salt and William Bankes. Having made local arrangements for the removal of the obelisk to the water's edge, Belzoni allowed his hired workmen to prepare unsupervised a jetty to enable the great shaft of stone to be loaded on a boat.

On my return, the pier appeared quite strong enough to bear at least forty times the weight it had to support; but, alas! when the obelisk came gradually on from the sloping bank, and all the weight rested on it, the pier, with the obelisk, and some of the men, took a slow movement, and majestically descended into the river, wishing us better success. I was not three yards off when this happened, and for some minutes, I must confess, I remained as stiff as a post. The first thing that came into my head, was the loss of such a piece of antiquity . . .

A mishap of this kind represented but a minor setback to the resourceful Belzoni, but before he had any chance to plan the salvage of the monument he had to deal with Mr Bankes:

I believe he was not less displeased than myself when I saw the accident, and on his arrival he said, that such things would happen sometimes; but I saw that he was not in a careful humour himself, so I informed him that the obelisk was not lost, and that in two or three days it would be on board.

And so it was; and in due course it passed safely through the rapids, down the Nile to Alexandria, and eventually to England. It was then that the hieroglyphic and Greek inscriptions on this obelisk were examined by Bankes and by Thomas Young, the English physicist, who had already made significant advances in the decipherment of the Egyptian scripts. Using results obtained from study of the texts on the Rosetta Stone, Young was able to identify the cartouche containing the name Cleopatra, here not the famous but ill-fated Cleopatra, but the consort of Ptolemy VII, Euergetes II, and the third Ptolemaic queen so named.

The river journey south from Philae was, before the building of the dams, an extraordinary progression from temple to temple. Many were small, but others were of very respectable size; some were architecturally of great interest, and often beautifully sited; others represented extraordinary feats of engineering. Even up to the time when work began on the High Dam, in the early 1960s, it was still possible to obtain an impression of Lower Nubia which retained something of its ancient flavour. The Nile itself, much wider than its natural channel for much of the year, still gave some impression of being a river, even though it had been transformed into a fairly substantial lake at the Aswan end. It did not spread deep into the hills on the east and west as it does today behind the infinitely greater High Dam. Those same hills formed the new shores of the widened river and they were still occupied by the clean and picturesque villages of the indigenous Nubians. Spectacular dunes of golden sand poured down to the water's edge and from time to time there were trees and cultivated fields where enough fertile silt had been deposited between high and low water-lines. Up to the late 1960s it was still possible to visit many of the temples which had been built in Lower Nubia in antiquity. It is still something of a mystery why these temples were placed in a region devoid of a settled Egyptian population, where there were no substantial towns apart, perhaps, from Aniba, the administrative capital of the region in the New Kingdom and the seat of the Viceroy of Kush.

The generally accepted view is that successive Egyptian kings regarded the building of

temples and shrines in Nubia as a means of impressing on the local inhabitants that there was more to Egyptian domination than the presence of administrative and military officials, and the imposition of controls and taxes. In the case of Ramesses II there was in addition the wish to establish the divinity of the living Pharaoh; the same intention can be detected in the constructions of the Graeco-Roman Period. Apart from Abu Simbel, the largest temple in the region was at Kalabsha, built by the Emperor Augustus and dedicated to the the Nubian deity Mandulis. It takes the form of the conventional Egyptian temple with a fine pylon, wide open forecourt, hypostyle hall and a series of rooms approaching the sanctuary. The last, as is the case in many Nubian temples, was converted into a church in the early Christian period. Kalabsha temple, along with other substantial monuments, has now been re-erected on a site just to the south of the High Dam on the west side of the great lake. Similar groupings of moved temples are now to be found at two other places to the south.

At the first grouping, about one hundred miles to the south, the principal building is the temple of Ramesses II formerly sited at Wadi es-Sebua ('Valley of the lions'). In its ancient position, still well remembered, it was approached by an avenue of sphinxes wearing double crowns, all badly silted up, emerging from their muddy encumbrances in various stages of picturesque decay. It was for them that the 'Valley of the lions' was named. The temple proper has two standing colossi of the king before the entrance to the principal court, and beyond it the expected hypostyle and suite of rooms surrounding and enclosing the sanctuary are unexpectedly cut into the living rock.

Two other much later temples are grouped with the Ramesses II temple, still, though quite incongruously, called Wadi es-Sebua. In the second grouping, about another twenty-five miles further upstream, there are again two temples and a tomb. Of the temples the more interesting is that known as Amada, built in the Eighteenth Dynasty, and the earliest well-preserved structure in Lower Nubia. In its original location it lay low on the water's edge, scarcely visible from a distance so well did it merge with its hilly background. It was built partly by Tuthmosis III and partly by his son Amenophis II, and a court was added by their successor Tuthmosis IV. Its reliefs are of a much higher artistic quality than, and far superior in execution to, what may be seen in most Nubian temples in this Egyptian stretch of Nubia. They have, however, been disfigured to some extent by the royal agents of Akhenaten who sought out and destroyed representations of the god Amon-Re, and cut out his divine names wherever they existed throughout metropolitan

**139** David Roberts' engraving of the building known as Trajan's kiosk, or 'Pharaoh's Bedstead', part of the complex of Philae as it could be seen before the building of the Aswan Dam.

**140** Nile scene in Nubia, with the hill of Qasr Ibrim on the left: a coloured engraving by David Roberts.

Egypt, and even here in extra-territorial Nubia. Many reliefs in the area of the sanctuary were much later plastered over and painted with Christian scenes.

The tomb which has been transferred from its original site to take its new place with the temples of Amada and Derr (yet another rock-cut shrine of the reign of Ramesses II), was cut for Penne who was in effect the Viceroy of Kush in the reign of Ramesses VI of the Twentieth Dynasty (c. 1151–1143 BC), although he is not himself given the formal title in his tomb inscriptions. Historically, and religiously, the most interesting scene among the surviving ritual decorations depicts the worshipping of the statue of Ramesses VI, a graphic demonstration of the survival of an active royal cult in Nubia. In general Egyptians did not like being buried away from their home districts in Egypt itself, but there is much evidence of a large Egyptian cemetery in the neighbourhood of Aniba from which Penne's tomb has been moved. We have already mentioned that Aniba was the centre of Egyptian administration in Lower Nubia, and it must be supposed that the establishment of a long-lasting and large Egyptian outpost here created a kind of Egyptian enclave of so settled a character that it could be regarded almost as a part of the 'real' Egypt.

Up to the time of the flooding of Lower Nubia, Aniba remained a settlement of some size, supported by a large (by Nubian standards) cultivated district. All has now disappeared beneath the waters of Lake Nasser, a fate that has mercifully not been suffered by the fortress of Qasr Ibrim, opposite Aniba on the east bank of the Nile. Here on the top of a lofty bluff overlooking the river stood a fortified site which dominated this part of Nubia from Pharaonic times down to the early nineteenth century. It is the only ancient site of any consequence in Lower Nubia to have escaped flooding, and it now survives as an island on the east side of Lake Nasser, but sometimes united to the eastern shore by a neck of land when the level of the waters falls, as it has done since the early 1980s.

Qasr Ibrim may first have carried a fortified position in the mid-Eighteenth Dynasty, but the evidence so far unearthed by excavations remains inconclusive in this respect. It was certainly occupied in the Twenty-fifth Dynasty when kings of Nubian origin invaded Egypt and usurped the royal power. Subsequently it remained a place of great importance, site of pagan Meroïtic and Roman temples and settlements; possibly the capital city of a people of uncertain origin which controlled this region in the fifth to seventh centuries AD (known enigmatically as the X-group, but possibly to be identified as the barbarous Blemmyes); the seat of a bishopric and site of a cathedral down to the fourteenth century; and finally the garrison town of a Bosnian occupation force, established in the early sixteenth century by the Turkish Sultan Selim. The Bosnian garrison, or its descendant force, remained until it was driven out by the Mamelukes fleeing from the wrath of Muhammad Ali in 1812. Destroyed and abandoned, Qasr Ibrim remained a site of infinite archaeological potential which was first systematically investigated by British excavators in the early 1960s as part of the great Nubian Rescue programme. In later years the excavation became substantially a joint British-American project.

Rain scarcely ever falls in this Nubian region, and exceptionally dry conditions prevail at Qasr Ibrim. In consequence, almost everything made of organic materials has escaped destruction in the many levels of occupation which extend back almost continuously for

140

at least 2,500 years. In the course of twenty-five years' excavation huge quantities of textiles, basket-work, sandals, and documents on papyrus, leather, vellum and paper have been recovered. The documents are remarkable, including texts in ancient Egyptian (various scripts), Meroïtic, Greek, Latin, Old Nubian, Coptic, Arabic and Turkish. There are liturgical texts, biblical texts (in different languages), business documents and hundreds of letters, the last especially from the time of the Bosnian occupation. There are more documentary texts in Meroïtic and Old Nubian than have ever been previously discovered; there is a Latin poem by Cornelius Gallus, the first Governor of Roman Egypt, a letter in indifferent Greek from a king of the Blemmyes to a rival king of the Nobatai, seeking the return of territory, the Letters Testimonial confirming the appointment of Timotheus as Bishop at Ibrim in 1372; and much else that illuminates the life and history of the communities which occupied this distant outpost. To supplement the documents (if one may put it this way round, instead of the other, more usual way) there are substantial physical remains of the buildings of the successive occupations: not only religious buildings of the many different faiths, from Twenty-fifth Dynasty temple to Islamic mosque, but well preserved houses, administrative buildings, a drinking establishment, fortifications of a monumental character. In addition pottery and metalwork in large quantities and even some woodwork are found at all levels, although the last is not so common, as wood, precious in this arid land, tended to be used again and again before being burnt as fuel. Much remains to be discovered in this fascinating place.

Not quite thirty miles to the south of Qasr Ibrim, but on the west bank of the river, are the two temples of Abu Simbel, both built in the reign of Ramesses II, the smaller of which honours the goddess Hathor along with Ramesses' great wife Nofretari. The larger, in which Ramesses himself is accorded divine honours along with Re-Herakhty, Amon-Re and Ptah, is one of the most striking and memorable of Egyptian temples, and undoubtedly the magnet which will draw the interested visitor south of Aswan. But now, as most people know, the temples have been raised high above their former positions to a plateau well out of reach of the waters of Lake Nasser.

Even after the building of the first Aswan dam and its first heightenings, the Abu Simbel temples were a fair distance from the river. Baedeker in 1929 specified a walk of about five minutes from boat to temple 'across the fields'. In the years just before the building of the High Dam, the river came within a few hundred yards of the great statues of the main temple, and almost lapped the façade of Nofretari's temple. Then one could admire the dawn standing on the deck of the Sudanese post-boat, coming straight from one's cabin, warmly wrapped in heavy coat over night wear; for the notice on board did say 'pyjamas not to be worn on deck'.

The first European who recorded seeing the site was the great and intrepid Swiss traveller Jean-Louis Burckhardt, and it was he who inspired Belzoni to visit the place and penetrate the great blanketing sand-dunes to enter the imposing hypostyle hall, the vestibule and the shrine, all of which are cut deep into the sandstone hill. The same sand-dunes which concealed much of the façade also enabled visitors to climb up the northernmost colossus and carve their names on the exposed surfaces within reach. The sand also allowed Robert Hay, the famous Scottish antiquarian, who came to Abu Simbel in the 1830s, to take a huge plaster mould of the face of the northern colossus,

141 *(overleaf)* Nubia before the flooding caused by the High Dam. The temple of Amada, seen in the centre, has now been moved to higher ground above the waters of Lake Nasser.

from which a cast was subsequently made for exhibition in the British Museum. It was last shown in the late 1960s at the time of the so-called Nubian Emergency; at over 11 feet high, and raised on a substantial plinth, it dominated all other Egyptian sculpture, large and small, in its neighbourhood.

When Miss Amelia Edwards came to Abu Simbel in 1874 she was put out by the many blobs of plaster-of-Paris left from Hay's moulding operations, and she set her sailors to work to remedy the disfigurements:

A scaffolding of spars and oars was at once improvised, and the men, delighted as children at play, were soon swarming all over the huge head, just as the carvers may have swarmed over it in the days when Rameses was king.

All they had to do was to remove any small lumps that might yet adhere to the surface, and then tint the white patches with coffee . . .

Rameses' appetite for coffee was prodigious. He consumed I know not how many gallons in a day. Our cook stood aghast at the demand made upon his stores. Never before had he been called upon to provide for a guest whose mouth measured three feet and a half in width.

The drawing accompanying this account shows the sailors perched on the scaffold and on suitable surfaces of the head, while in the foreground, high on the sand dune, the author is shown seated beneath a parasol sketching the view, while her companion makes comments on the results.

Less than twenty miles south of Abu Simbel is the modern frontier between Egypt and the Sudan, a political rather than a true geographical frontier. Before the creation of Lake Nasser, the Nubian race straddled the line, and the subsequent separation of those who were politically Egyptian from those who were Sudanese was a sad and painful consequence of the flooding of their lands and villages. In antiquity there was no frontier here, and the nations and peoples which occupied the region at different periods extended their control indifferently to the north and to the south. The Egyptians, who are the principal actors in this account of the land and its monuments, clearly found the region to the south, especially in the neighbourhood of the second cataract, crucial for the control of traffic from the south, whether for trade or for hostile purposes. In consequence a series of strategically sited forts was constructed in the Middle Kingdom to provide control points and to accommodate garrisons. They were remarkably substantial strongholds, although built of unbaked mud-brick for the most part, with many defensive features which were to form the characteristic elements of medieval European castles; great enclosure walls, bastions, battlements, moats, drawbridges, ramparts, linked embrasures for cross-fire by archers. Inside the walls there were quarters for the garrisons, storerooms, houses and offices for administrative staff, all laid out in a rough grid pattern of streets. In the great fort at Buhen there were also temples, although the buildings which survived up to the flooding by Lake Nasser were of New Kingdom date. The largest of all the fortresses was at Mirgissa, a few miles to the south of the old town of Wadi Halfa, formerly the terminus of the railway from Khartoum. Identified as the ancient Iken, Mirgissa was revealed in the excavations which took place during the Nubian Emergency as probably the most important of the forts from the administrative point of view, serving as the main depot for goods brought from the south to be imported into Egypt.

The most southerly of the Middle Kingdom forts in the second cataract region was at

142 Amelia Edwards sketches at Abu Simbel while her sailors clamber over scaffolding to scour one of the royal heads.

Semna, about forty miles upstream from Wadi Halfa. A taste of the business carried on at this important control-point may be gained from a document which was found at Thebes but which contains transcripts of dispatches sent from Semna in the reign of King Ammenemes III of the Twelfth Dynasty (*c.* 1844–1797 BC). They are concerned mostly with the vetting of Medjay, the nomadic inhabitants of the region to the east and south, some of whom clearly sought entry into Egypt, usually on false pretexts. The papyrus is poorly preserved, but something has been made of those parts in reasonable condition:

Six more Nubians reached the fort 'Khakaure-is-mighty' [Semna] to carry on trade like this . . ., on the 8th day of the 4th month of the winter season. They traded what they had brought and went back south to the place from which they had come, on this day.

Kindly note that 2 of the Medjay men and 3 women . . . came down from the desert on the 27th day of the 3rd month of winter in regnal year 3 [of Ammenemes III]. They said; 'We have come to serve the Great House (may it live, be prosperous and healthy)'. They were asked about the state of the desert and they said 'We have not heard everything; but the desert is dying of famine'. So they said. Then this servant [i.e. the writer of the dispatch] had them sent back to their desert on this day.

A line or two at the end of this last dispatch contains an obscure objection raised by two of the Medjay. It is clear that they had good reason to enter Egypt, in view of the drought in their own land, and were being refused accordingly. Old problems tend to recur in this part of the world; the plight of these Medjay is reflected in recent famines in the Sudan.

In later times the Medjay were to be rather more appreciated by the Egyptians, to be recruited as mercenaries and widely used as police during the New Kingdom. Things had changed markedly in Egypt's relations with Nubia from the Seventeenth Dynasty onwards. The Nubian princedom of Kush in Lower Nubia was allied with the alien Hyksos, and only by chance was prevented from joining the struggle which eventually led to the expulsion of the Hyksos in the early years of the Eighteenth Dynasty. The presence of an actively hostile state to the south of Elephantine could not be tolerated, and swift and firm action was taken to re-establish the influence of the Theban kings over Lower Nubia and well to the south. In consequence Egyptian forces penetrated much deeper to the south, at least as far as the fourth cataract, and established in the Eighteenth Dynasty their southernmost outpost, Napata, just short of the cataract and under the shadow of the isolated and imposing Gebel Barkal. Fortified settlements were established at many sites between the second and third cataracts, and also to the south of the third cataract, but not in such numbers as further north.

Temples of some size were constructed in many of these settlements, the most spectacular and best preserved being at Soleb, built in the reign of Amenophis III and dedicated to Amun and the king himself. Among the distinguished monuments which once graced this temple were two granite lions, which were subsequently moved to Gebel Barkal and are described a little later in this chapter. Amenophis III also built at Sedeinga, a few miles downstream, a temple dedicated to his wife, Queen Tiye, and another at Sesebi to the south of Soleb. Sesebi, however, is remarkable for a triple temple dedicated to the Aten by Amenophis IV early in his reign, before he changed his name to Akhenaten. In the aftermath of the short-lived Atenist revolution, this building was usurped and modified in the reign of Sethos I. Even in far-away Nubia, the religious passions of the counter-revolution were vented on the memorials of the luckless

Akhenaten. There is surprisingly no trace of him at Kawa, a place almost 100 miles upstream from Sesebi which in the Eighteenth Dynasty was named Gempaten ('the Aten is perceived'). It might be thought that a new settlement so named would have been founded in Akhenaten's reign, but the earliest buildings there seem to date to the reign of Tutankhamun. In spite of its pregnant meaning, the name persisted down to the Twenty-fifth Dynasty when it was shortened to Gematen in the reign of Taharqa (c. 690–664 BC). He was one of the Kushite dynasty of kings based at Napata which conducted a crusade in the name of Amon-Re to purge Egypt and rehabilitate the ancient temples of the land.

Two granite sculptures from Kawa which encapsulate the vigour of Taharqa and the religious zeal of the Kushite or Napatan Dynasty are a small sphinx with a head in the likeness of the king and a colossal ram with a small figure of the king standing between its forelegs. The former takes up the idea of king as sphinx smiting his enemies, an image employed by Taharqa in the reliefs of his Kawa temple. In form and style it harks back to sphinxes of the Middle Kingdom, but the face of Taharqa is individual, strong, even brutal in its realistic portrayal of this single-minded king. The second sculpture resumes strikingly the iconography of the rams which form some of the processional avenues at Thebes. This animal represented one of the natural forms of appearance (theophanies, as they are sometimes grandly called) of the god Amon-Re, and here the god, as ram, protects King Taharqa. This sculpture, one of four which originally stood in front of the pylon of the Kawa temple founded by Taharqa himself, is a majestic image of divinity protecting royalty in the direct line of Egyptian tradition.

The phenomenon of the survival of the worship of Amon-Re at Napata for centuries after the departure of the last native Egyptian garrison is unexplained. Nevertheless, the indigenous kingdom established there by Nubian rulers and usually called Kushite, or Napatan (and even

143 Upper part of a granite colossus of Ramesses II represented with the royal insignia of crook and flail: from the temple of Khnum on Elephantine.

Ethiopian, to use the terminology of the Egyptian historian Manetho), continued and promoted with extraordinary devotion the cult of the Theban deity. In due course, for reasons among which were undoubtedly missionary zeal and political advantage, a successful attempt was made to take over Egypt, to revitalise the ancient cults, particularly that of Amon-Re, and to establish the Kushite rulers as Kings of Upper and Lower Egypt, to be the successors of the Pharaohs who were the great promoters of the Theban deities during the New Kingdom.

At Napata, the evidence of the power and influence of the Kushite kings, stemming from before the invasion of Egypt and lasting well into the fourth century BC is amply visible in the form of cemeteries and temple buildings. It is not our purpose here to trace the subsequent history of the Kushite rulers, or to follow them when their capital was transferred to Meroë, about 350 miles upstream, just beyond the confluence of the Atbara with the Nile. But it may be of interest to note the extent to which a vestigial attachment to Egypt persisted for many centuries after the withdrawal in 656 BC of the last Kushite king of the Twenty-fifth Dynasty, Tantamani. At the religious centre of Kushite power, in the shadow of Gebel Barkal, the evidence of the temple buildings erected by the Kushite kings shows an attachment to the hieroglyphic script which lasted long after the demise of those who clearly understood how to express themselves in the Egyptian language, at least in its monumental form. The Nubians may not have been good linguists (remember the indifferent Greek of the letter written by the King of the Blemmyes, found at Qasr Ibrim), but at least they tried.

The grandest temple building at Gebel Barkal was started in the reign of Tuthmosis III and added to greatly by the kings of the Nineteenth Dynasty; it received further additions in the reign of Piye (Piankhi), the conqueror of Egypt, and was reconstructed by King Natakamani in the early first century AD; in all a building history of about 1,500 years. Other temple buildings were inaugurated in the time of the early Kushite/Twenty-fifth Dynasty rulers, and subsequently. Following the tradition of Egyptian kings, although probably not consciously, sculptures from New Kingdom temples downstream were brought to embellish Kushite constructions. Of these the two most striking are the granite lions from Soleb, which were mentioned earlier. The inscriptions carved on them reveal quite a chequered history, one being probably a little older in date than the other. One is inscribed with a text in which Amenophis III states explicitly that the statue was made 'as his monument of his living image upon earth . . . dwelling in the fortress Khaemma'at (Soleb)'; on the breast are the cartouches of the Kushite, or more probably Meroïtic, King Amanislo (297–284 BC) who still, quite falsely and anachronistically, uses the Egyptian royal titles 'King of Upper and Lower Egypt' and 'Son of Re'. The second lion is inscribed principally with a text in which Tutankhamun is stated to have 'renewed the monuments of his father Amenophis III'; here 'father' probably means 'forbear' or 'ancestor'. The text on the breast of this lion names a king, probably Ay, the ephemeral successor of Tutankhamun, who claims to have 'brought it'; by which it is probably meant that it was Ay who installed the lion at Soleb after Tutankhamun's untimely death, placing it in company with the earlier lion which had presumably been installed in its position in the reign of Amenophis III. On this second lion the names of Amanislo, the Meroïte, are cut on the left paw. It is generally thought that it was Amanislo who had the lions removed from Soleb to Gebel Barkal, confirming his action by having his 'false'

144 Excavations in the fortress of Buhen, built in the Middle Kingdom and reconstructed in the Eighteenth Dynasty; now under the waters of Lake Nasser.

145 Part of a relief from the pyramid chapel of Queen Shanakdakhete at Meroë: she is shown here receiving offerings and protected by the goddess Isis.

148

146 The statue of the Lady Sennuy, found in her husband's tomb at Kerma in Nubia: a remarkable sculpture of the early Twelfth Dynasty.

147 Granite sphinx from the temple of Kawa in Nubia. The head represents King Taharqa of the Twenty-fifth Dynasty.

148 One of the two granite lions from Gebel Barkal, made originally for the temple at Soleb. This lion carries a text of King Tutankhamun.

cartouche carved on both. He chose well, for these noble beasts are among the finest animal sculptures from any culture, ancient or modern. In the early nineteenth century the lions were on the move again, taken to England by the first Lord Prudhoe (later 4th Duke of Northumberland) who built up a large and important collection of Egyptian antiquities at Alnwick Castle, now mostly in the Oriental Museum of the University of Durham. The lions were presented to the British Museum in 1835.

Egypt continued to be the inspiration for the decorations carved in the tombs and temples of the Kushite rulers at Meroë itself and at the sites in the reaches of the Nile between the Atbara confluence and modern Khartoum. In the late second century BC, however, a significant change was signalled by the abandonment of Egyptian hieroglyphs for a new, derived, hieroglyphic script developed (with a cursive form) for the writing of the Meroïtic language itself. The earliest examples of the new script so far identified have been found on a monument of the reign of Queen Shanakdakhete. A wall from the chapel attached to her pyramid at the great royal cemetery at Meroë (modern Begrawiya) was presented to the British Museum by the Sudanese Government in 1905. 

145    It dates from the mid- to late-second century BC and shows the queen with a prince under the protection of the goddess Isis with outstretched wings – a common ancient Egyptian image, here somewhat stiffly interpreted. Five registers of offering bearers are to be seen approaching the queen and there are other smaller ritual scenes included in the general scheme. It is extraordinary to consider the tenacity with which these far distant, wholly alien, rulers clung to this graphic tradition which had its origins in the reliefs of the Egyptian temples of the New Kingdom in Nubia. Direct contacts between Meroë and Ptolemaic Egypt were perhaps greater than the evidence at present available to us will allow; but it would not be correct, except in the most tenuous way, to regard Meroë as the furthest outpost of Egyptian power to the south of Elephantine. It cannot be denied, however, that in Nubia Egypt secured through religion a continuity of influence which long outlasted her political attempts to control the country.

149 Bronze head of the Emperor Augustus, larger than life-size, found in excavations at Meroë. Its presence in this distant place has never been satisfactorily explained.

# BIBLIOGRAPHY

ADAMS, W.Y., *Nubia: Corridor to Africa*, Princeton, 1977.

ALDRED, C., *The Egyptians*, London, 1984.

ANDREWS, CAROL, *Egyptian Mummies*, London, 1984.

ANDREWS, CAROL, *The Rosetta Stone*, London, 1981.

BAEDEKER, K., *Egypt and the Sudan*, 8th ed., Leipzig, 1929. Reprint, Newton Abbott, 1974.

BAIKIE, J., *Egyptian Antiquities in the Nile Valley*, London, 1932.

BAINES, J. and MALEK, J., *Atlas of Ancient Egypt*, Oxford, 1978.

BALL, J., *Contributions to the Geography of Egypt*, Cairo, 1939.

BALL, J., *Egypt in the Classical Geographers*, Cairo, 1942.

BARGUET, P., *Le Temple d'Amon-Rê à Karnak*, Cairo, 1962.

BELZONI, G.-B., *Narrative of operations and recent discoveries within pyramids, temples, tombs and excavations in Egypt and Nubia*, 2 vols, London, 1821.

BIERBRIER, M., *The Tomb-Builders of the Pharaohs*, London, 1982.

BOWMAN, A.K., *Egypt after the Pharaohs*, London, 1986.

BUDGE, E.A.T.W., *By Nile and Tigris*, 2 vols, London, 1920.

BUTZER, K.W., *Early Hydraulic Civilization in Egypt*, Chicago and London, 1976.

CLARKE, S. and ENGELBACH, R., *Ancient Egyptian Masonry*, London, 1930.

DAVIES, W.V., *Egyptian Hieroglyphs*, London, 1987.

DROWER, M.S., *Flinders Petrie*, London, 1985.

DUFF GORDON, L., *Letters from Egypt*, London, 1865; new ed., London, 1983.

EDWARDS, AMELIA B., *A Thousand Miles up the Nile*, London, 1877; new ed., London, 1972.

EDWARDS, I.E.S., *The Pyramids of Egypt*, rev. ed., Harmondsworth, 1985.

FRASER, P.M., *Ptolemaic Alexandria*, 3 vols, Oxford, 1972.

GARDINER, A.H., *Ancient Egyptian Onomastica*, 3 vols, Oxford, 1947.

GARDINER, A.H., *Egypt of the Pharaohs*, Oxford, 1962.

GAUTHIER, H., *Dictionnaire des noms géographiques contenus dans les textes hiéroglyphiques*, 7 vols, Cairo, 1925–31.

HARRIS, J.R., ed., *The Legacy of Egypt*, Oxford, 1972.

HAYES, W.C., *The Scepter of Egypt*, 2 vols, New York, 1953, 1957.

HUME, W.F., *The Geology of Egypt*, 2 vols, Cairo, 1925, 1935.

JAMES, T.G.H., *The British Museum and Ancient Egypt*, London, 1982.

JAMES, T.G.H., *Egyptian Painting*, London, 1985.

JAMES, T.G.H., ed., *Excavating in Egypt*, London, 1984.

JAMES, T.G.H., ed., *An Introduction to Ancient Egypt*, London, 1979.

JAMES, T.G.H. and DAVIES, W.V., *Egyptian Sculpture*, London, 1983.

JEFFREYS, D.G., *The Survey of Memphis*, London, 1985.

KEES, H., *Ancient Egypt. A Cultural Topography*, London, 1961.

LAUER, J.-P., *Saqqara. The Royal Cemetery of Memphis*, London, 1976.

LICHTHEIM, M., *Ancient Egyptian Literature*, 3 vols, Berkeley and Los Angeles, 1973–80.

LUCAS, A., *Ancient Egyptian Materials and Industries*, 4th ed., rev. J.R. Harris, London, 1964.

MONTET, P., *Géographie de l'Egypte ancienne*, 2 vols, Paris, 1957, 1961.

MORET, A., *The Nile and Egyptian Civilisation*, London, 1927.

MURNANE, W.J., *A Penguin Guide to Ancient Egypt*, Harmondsworth, 1983.

NIMS, C.F., *Thebes of the Pharaohs*, London, 1965.

PORTER B. and MOSS, R.L.B., *Topographical Bibliography of Ancient Egyptian Hieroglyphical Texts, Reliefs and Paintings*, 7 vols, Oxford, 1927– (with revisions).

SMITH, W.S., *The Art and Architecture of Ancient Egypt*, 2nd ed., rev. W.K. Simpson, Harmondsworth, 1981.

SPENCER, A.J., *Death in Ancient Egypt*, Harmondsworth, 1982.

STEAD, MIRIAM, *Egyptian Life*, London, 1986.

WEIGALL, A.E.P., *Guide to the Antiquities of Upper Egypt from Abydos to the Sudan Frontier*, London, 1910.

WILKINSON, J.G., *The Manners and Customs of the Ancient Egyptians*, 3 vols, London, 1837; rev. S. Birch, London, 1878.

Relief figure of Ankhnesneferibre, God's Adorer of Amun in the late Twenty-sixth Dynasty, from her schist sarcophagus.

# PHOTOGRAPHIC ACKNOWLEDGEMENTS

Most of the photographs in this volume are reproduced from British Museum (BM) official negatives, the majority being the work of Mr Peter Hayman. Grateful thanks are also extended to the trustees and other governing bodies of the following institutions: the Museum of Fine Arts, Boston (MFA), the Metropolitan Museum of Art, New York (MMA), The Brooklyn Museum (TBM), the Egypt Exploration Society (EES), the National Gallery, London (NG), the National Trust (NT); and also to the private scholars and friends mentioned individually below. The maps are the skilled work of Christine Barratt.

*Half-title page:* MMA 31.3.157
*Title page:* Photo T.G.H. JAMES
*Contents page:* Photo EES
*Page 7:* Photo JOHN HEDGECOE
1 Photo T.G.H. JAMES
2 Photo A.K. BOWMAN
3 BM 20
4 From E.D. CLARKE, *The Tomb of Alexander* (Cambridge, 1805)
5 BM 55253
6 BM 24
7 Photo CAROL ANDREWS
8 Photo EES
9 BM 36346
10 BM 37977
11 BM 64391
12 Photo T.G.H. JAMES
13 BM 1063
14 BM 12337
15 BM 1077
16 BM GR 1888.6-1.456
17 Photo A.K. BOWMAN
18 Photo CAROL ANDREWS
19 BM 171
20 Photo A.J. SPENCER
21 BM 67186
22 BM 22920
23 Photo T.G.H. JAMES
24 BM 682
25 BM 36
26 BM 1181
27 Photo T.G.H. JAMES
28 BM 37883
29 BM 498
30 MMA 23.10.1
31 BM 17
32 BM 23

33 Photo T.G.H. JAMES
34 BM 6647
35 BM 29772
36 Photo T.G.H. JAMES
37 Photo TERESA FRANCIS
38 Photo MIRIAM STEAD
39 BM 52887
40 Photo BM of facsimile by NINA DAVIES
41 BM 69014
42 Photo T.G.H. JAMES
43 BM 55722
44 BM 1239
45 Photo DIANA JAMES
46 Photo T.G.H. JAMES
47 BM 15485, 37563
48 BM 21801
49 Photo DIANA JAMES
50 Photo R. COLES
51 NG 1266 on loan to BM. Photo A.K. BOWMAN
52 Photo T.G.H. JAMES
53 BM 68512
54 BM 59648
55 Photo T.G.H. JAMES
56 Photo MIRIAM STEAD
57 Photo EES
58 BM 1147
59 BM 46631
60 Photo BM of facsimile by NINA DAVIES
61 TBM 33.685
62 MFA 20.1822-1827
63 BM 57399
64 BM 55617
65 BM 55193
66 From a watercolour by H. CARR. Photo A.K. BOWMAN
67 Photo EES
68 BM 20717
69 Photo T.G.H. JAMES
70 Photo T.G.H. JAMES
71 BM 9524
72 BM 461
73 BM 569, 570
74 BM 55586
75 BM 37996
76 Photo EES
77 BM 947
78 Photo T.G.H. JAMES
79 BM 32639 (box), 58199 (painted jar), 53885 (jar with gekko)
80 Photo T.G.H. JAMES
81 BM 20790, 20792; cast of Louvre fragment, top right
82 BM 20791
83 Photo T.G.H. JAMES
84 BM 117
85 BM 37348
86 BM 60006
87 Photo T.G.H. JAMES

88 Reproduced by kind permission of Major J.G. CHESTER
89 Photo T.G.H. JAMES
90 BM 45, at present on loan to Memphis State University, Tennessee
91 BM 15, 55 (the arm)
92 Photo T.G.H. JAMES
93 BM 67969
94 BM 43
95 BM 61
96 BM 12
97 Photo T.G.H. JAMES
98 BM 75
99 BM 986
100 BM 1514
101 BM 480
102 BM 174
103 Photo T.G.H. JAMES
104 BM 38212
105 Photo T.G.H. JAMES
106 Photo MIRIAM STEAD
107 BM 9901, sheet 5
108 BM 2463
109 BM 37984
110 BM 29770
111 BM 10221
112 BM 882, 883, 48001 (coffin)
113 BM 10016
114 BM 683
115 Photo CAROL ANDREWS
116 BM 686
117 Photo T.G.H. JAMES
118 From Plates vol. of Belzoni's *Narrative*. BM 19
119 BM 4, 5
120 BM 614
121 Photo MIRIAM STEAD
122 Photo T.G.H. JAMES
123 Photo T.G.H. JAMES
124 Gardner Wilkinson Papers from Calke Abbey, Bodleian Library, Oxford (NT)
125 BM 47992
126 BM 1696
127 BM 10498
128 BM 32751
129 Photo T.G.H. JAMES
130 Photo A.K. BOWMAN
131 Photo T.G.H. JAMES
132 Photo A.K. BOWMAN
133 BM 98
134 Photo T.G.H. JAMES
135 Photo T.G.H. JAMES
136 Photo T.G.H. JAMES
137 BM 922
138 Photo A.K. BOWMAN
139 Photo A.K. BOWMAN
140 Photo A.K. BOWMAN
141 Photo DIANA JAMES
142 Reproduced from *A Thousand Miles up the Nile*

143 BM 67
144 Photo EES
145 BM 719
146 MFA 14.720
147 BM 1770
148 BM 2
149 BM GR 1911.9-1.1
*Page 218:* BM 32
*Page 222:* BM 9999, sheet 43
*Page 223:* BM 720

# INDEX

Painting of Sakhmet, consort of Ptah, the god of Memphis. From a vignette in the Great Harris Papyrus.

Painted sandstone head of King Nebhepetre Mentuhotpe II, from Deir el-Bahri.